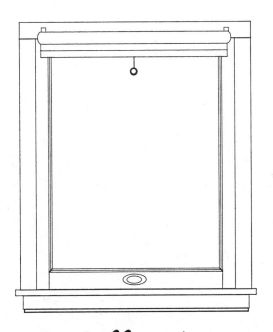

the hilltop heart

REFLECTIONS OF A PRACTICAL MYSTIC

the hilltop heart

REFLECTIONS OF A PRACTICAL MYSTIC

JAMES DILLET FREEMAN

Unity Books
Unity Village, MO 64065

The Hilltop Heart was originally published by
Doubleday & Company, Inc.
under the title
Happiness Can Be a Habit.

Front cover photograph by Tony Griffiths
Text and cover designed by Linda Gates

Published by Unity School of Christianity
Unity Village, MO 64065

Second Printing 1993

LLC 91-066453
ISBN 0-87159-050-6
Canada GST R132529033

*To the angels who occasionally sing in me
when I manage
to rise to the top of my heart.*

TABLE OF CONTENTS

| ONE | *a world of purpose and beauty* | 13 |

| TWO | *world of atoms—world of faith* | 39 |

When you change, the world changes
Consider, for instance, walls
Seeing the spiritual reality
The power to touch reality

With what measure will you measure?
Life is what you make it
This is an enchanted world
Whatever you think it is, it is something more
Truth always happens
Not by our narrow notions
A clean slate
A city called Kansas City
Refuse to accept, decline to be bound
No easy formulas, no certain ways
More than we settle for

One morning in my garden
Life is a mystery
The work of a master artist
The sea calls to the sailor
You have come up to here
When one is infinitely dear
His sparrow . . . His star
The I of me

A divine economy
"Give, and it will be given"
The universe gives
The river at his root
Of eating and drinking
We are not splinter people
That the greater may come forth
Not by dying, but by love

Life is a dance
God is joy
As a root to water
We need not accept
Even when we cannot play the notes
The posture of joy
Love is joy

A vision of perfection
The perfect seed
The joy of a journey
A world so good
Not a one-note world
What would you have me be?

What would you like to be like?
On a Friday morning
Good shall be victorious
Death is not death
Perfect Man, come forth

Why do we make God less than we are?
As to Heaven
A vision of Hell
We are our own gatekeepers
You can never go back
You are what you are
Because we are good
Our spirit is like water
In the pattern of greatness
Aim beyond your reach
How good, how gentle we can be
The image of the Infinite
Something better than I dream

The work of love and intelligence
A single page, a single chord
To believe we are immortal
Every person feels he or she is immortal
More than he values life

If the slayer thinks he slays
To justify the injustices
We have lived before
A world governed by law

Why we have the life we have
Life is effort
A fish not even gold
The water comes down at Niagara Falls
How hard it is to be human
The end of the book

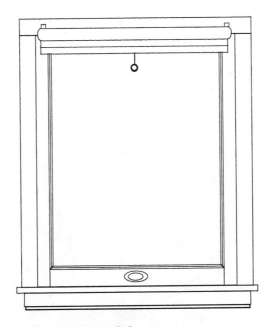

the hilltop heart

REFLECTIONS OF A PRACTICAL MYSTIC

the hilltop heart

If only you have a hilltop heart,
Life's compass points lie far apart;
What heights and deeps life has, how far
The hilltop heart's horizons are!
Hills have a way of stretching minds;
Lured-on imagination winds
Up over crests and down through hollows.
Hills tug at the heart, and the heart follows,
Dares the undared, tries the untried.
Hills always have another side;
If you make the climb up and descent,
You may find the valley of content.
Though a hilltop heart may never stand still,
Yet the heart was meant for the top of a hill!

The Hilltop Heart was published twenty-five years ago by Doubleday under another title. I don't like to title what I write because I don't know what it may say to you, so I told the publishers to title the book—they probably would have anyway—and they named it *Happiness Can Be a Habit.* That makes it the most mistitled book since the Phoenicians invented the alphabet.

My book is more poetry than prose, so I thought, Why not find a poetic title for it? I took a book of my poems and began to read off the titles, and when I came to "The Hilltop Heart," the editor said, "That's it. Your book is a look at the world and life from a higher perspective, that is, from a hilltop heart." So that is how it got its new title.

When I wrote the book, I told friends I was writing a poor man's *Paradise Lost.* Milton said he wrote his epic poem to "justify the ways of God to men." This is the age of doubt. There has never been a time when so many people have been asking, "Is it possible to believe that this world is the work of a God who is intelligence and love?" A considerable part of this book is my attempt to convince myself—and you—that this is such a world.

The editors thought that you might like to know how I came to write the book.

An editor who had bought a number of my poems for *McCall's* went to work for Doubleday. She had told me that I ought to try to get a book published, so I sent her some of the poems and essays I had written for *Daily Word.* She wrote back that she only handled women's fiction—Doubleday had sixty editors—but she would send my material to the editor who handled inspirational and religious writing. He sent my writing back saying that he was not interested in things I had already written, but thought I could write a book—would I send him an outline? I did this. He wrote back that he could see I did not know how to write an outline, but he still thought I could write a book. So I did.

It took me about a year. I was extremely busy at Unity at the time, so I wrote when I could, usually no more than a short passage. Oh, I don't mean that this writing was hard. Actually, a great deal of this book came rushing out of me; I could not write fast enough to get it down. The Foreword tells how I wrote the best parts of it.

Poets are not paid much, but sometimes when you write you get very high. When you stop writing, the creative energy does not stop flowing in you. This is one of the rewards of writing poetry.

One evening after I had been writing some part of the book, I got in bed with my wife and I turned to her and said, "You know, honey, I'm a very lucky guy. Angels sing in me." "Angels sing in me," I thought, "What a good line!" Then a second line came, "I rush to write down what I hear." I got out of bed, went back to my desk and wrote what became the Foreword to the book. When Unity told me they would like to bring the book out under a new title, I thought I would probably rewrite a lot of it. However, as I read, I became aware of something that I had not realized before. My book is not a metaphysical essay; it is a metaphysical poem—or, maybe it is better to say, a number of poems. My writing was not the work of my logical mind conforming to an outline. The writing was inspired. It came out of me, as the Foreword says, "in bits and snatches—hardly a few notes together." Then I had to piece into a book these phrases and lines that my angels sang. In the process, the heavenly sounds have been strung together on earthly ones—the angel song with my own.

How did the bits and snatches of the book come? I was mowing and my mower killed a snake. I walked to all four corners of my yard and I asked God to bless every living thing in it. And God said to me, "What is not a living thing?" Then I wrote "One morning in my garden."

I found the "fish not even gold," just as I say, on a cold March morning. My wife took him to Silent Unity and told his story at a meeting. She named him Junior Miracle.

The cherry tree I describe in "Life is effort" is still growing in my yard. It split again a few years ago and put forth yet another shoot, and is still bearing white blooms, red cherries—and courage.

One evening as my wife and I were getting ready for a party, I lay down on a couch to rest while she finished dressing and suddenly "A vision of perfection" was in my head. I only had to get up and write it down as fast as I could.

Another evening, I woke from sleep, saw Cerberus' three heads glaring at me, and wrote the vision I had of hell.

I thought I had finished "The I of me" when I wrote the paragraph, "Conceive if you can, something that is like a diamond . . . and just as much like a river . . . and you have caught a sense of the I of me." Then, as I came walking out of a prayer meeting, the rest of the piece came singing into my head. Sometimes people ask me what is my favorite piece of my writing. I can't answer that. But I will say the brief passage that begins with "Perhaps I am most like a song" and ends with "Listen!" will always be high among them.

When the sentence came to me that opens the passage "We are not splinter people," it almost made me quit writing the book. The sentence is, "This is a world where nothing lives but something dies." As I realized how true this is, I thought, how can I write a book saying that a world where this seems to be the universal rule can be the work of a God who is intelligence and love? It was weeks later—I believe it was on Easter Sunday—that the second truth came to me, "This is a world where nothing lives but something dies. But it is also a world where nothing dies but something lives!" Then, as in a revelation, I saw that we are not little, lonely, frightened, separate selves; we find our meaning as leaves find their meaning in a tree, or waves in a sea, or sparks in a fire, or notes in a symphony. Woven into the warp and woof of things, we are part of a universal process and divine economy, and we find our meaning in our oneness with the One.

After the book was published, I was on a radio show in Detroit. The young man—he told me he was a Catholic—who interviewed me said that when the publishers sent him the book, he did not read it. It sounded like a self-help, positive-thinking book and he had had enough of those. But since he had to talk to me about it, he finally thought he had better take a look at the book. "It isn't like I had thought at all," he said. "I keep my copy of the book by our bed and I read a part of it every night to my wife before we fall asleep." I have met other people who told me similar stories about how they read the book. Poetry is meant to be read aloud—you don't have to read it that way, but it helps.

So I have rewritten as little of the book as I could. You cannot rewrite a poem. Once in awhile you may change a word or two, but that is all. If I have not said all I hope to say—and may that always be the case!—let me write another poem; or perhaps even a metaphysical essay or two, though I would rather write poems. As for now, this is the song my angels sang for me—or at least this is how I interpreted their singing. I am listening. I pray that you will hear their singing, too, and that you will find, as I have, that this world of God's is a work of intelligence and love.

FOREWORD

Angels sing in me.

I rush to write down what I hear.

I carry a pad and pencil everywhere, for this singing may come at any hour in any place.

I must get it down quickly and turn it into words and phrases before it passes away, leaving no trace.

For the angels, I have noticed, hardly ever sing the same song twice—like God, they are original spirits and do not repeat themselves.

Usually the music comes in bursts and snatches—hardly a few notes together—a phrase, a line—that is all.

And I must turn this celestial strain I have caught, as the angels flew through my head, into a poem or a paragraph or even pages of writing.

This is hard.

The heavenly sounds get mixed with earthly ones—the angel song with my own.

All I can do is pray that my angels will return and look over my shoulder where I write and whisper a few more words in my ear.

So that the singing I heard you may hear too, for I pity all in this world who never hear an angel singing.

a world of purpose and beauty

ONE

"In the beginning God"

In the beginning God, having caused a Man and a Woman to be, saw after a while that the Man and Woman were ready to go forth to work out their destiny.

So God called the Man and the Woman to Him and held out two cups.

And God said, "Before you go, my children, come and drink with me. Here are two cups. The one cup is called Bliss and the other cup is called Effort. Choose now which cup you will drink from and I will drink from the cup you do not choose."

Then the Man and the Woman looked at God, who had made them. They looked at the world, which God also had made. And they saw that God had labored very hard.

Then they thought, "God is very, very old and all alone, and He has worked for eternity. And we are young and strong and have each other, and eternity lies all before us."

And they felt moved for God, for God had made them in His image, which is a Mind to Love.

So the two took the cup that God had called Effort and drank from it as if they were one.

Then God drank from the cup which He had called Bliss. But the last drops He spilt on His fingers and sprinkled over the Man and the Woman. And God blessed them, and they went forth hand in hand to find their destiny.

After that God stood alone and smiled. For God knew that Man's effort is his bliss and Man's bliss is his effort.

A long road from heaven

It is a long road from heaven to earth and back again.

Today we stand at a bewildered moment.

We have eaten of the Tree of Knowledge and the fruit has stuck in our throats.

This fruit should bring fat for our bones and fire for our veins—but halfway swallowed, it is choking us.

In the East there is a saying that when we have no knowledge of truth, mountains are mountains, rivers are rivers, trees are trees. When we get a little knowledge of truth, mountains are no longer mountains, rivers are no longer rivers, trees are no longer trees. But when we come into a full knowledge of truth, mountains are again mountains, rivers are again rivers, trees are again trees.

Today, we—we in the West, at least—stand at the second stage of the transformation. We have tasted the fruit of the tree, the scales have dropped from our eyes, and we see that the old, easy, cherished beliefs of our childhood centuries can no longer be believed.

So we don our white, aseptic laboratory gowns and cry out as with a revelation: "All truth is illusion. Nothing at all makes sense."

The world—our savants teach us—is a chemical accident, an electric sea, mysterious and imponderable but with no more meaning than a wave or a wind that rises and will pass away.

Life, too, is a chemical accident. It, too, has no meaning. Brief and full of pain, it ends with death.

The human being is, of course, part of the chemical accident. He is an animal, a rapacious animal. He, too, has no meaning. His mind an ingenious electrical circuit, his spirit a childish invention, he, too, ends with death.

The world, life, the human being—they are all to be explained in terms of physical law, mechanical principles.

There is, naturally, no God.

Truly, the mountains are no longer mountains.

A time of revolt

We live in a new age of reason that has become a revolt against reason. A revolt against beauty. A revolt against joy.

Artists dribble paint out of paint cans onto canvas. Sculptors weld together pieces of old iron and concrete that they have scavenged from a junkyard. Musicians blow Klaxons and bang tire irons for symphonies. Poets babble trivial obfuscations. Philosophers prove by reason that reason can prove nothing.

Life has no meaning, people say. Life has no meaning!

Especially the intellectual people say this. Sophisticated people. Educated people. The people who read books–even more, the people who write them—the artists and scientists and teachers and scholars.

The big-city people who have gone to the right schools.

The comfortable people—with light for night and heat for winter and cool for summer, with cars and planes and elevators to whisk them up and down and back and forth wherever they wish to go.

The insulated people with money in the bank, every risk insured, and a friendly loan waiting from the friendly lending agency.

The people with a medicine cabinet stuffed with tranquilizer pills, pep pills, pain-killing pills, sleeping pills, and pills to keep awake by.

The most secure people, the most fortunate people who have ever lived.

Life makes no sense, these people like to say.

The French Revolutionists put a statue of the Goddess of Reason in the temple and worshiped her. After that, Goya created his print *The Dream of Reason Produces Monsters.*

But the Dream of Unreason produces monstrosities—and that is no better.

We human beings have unreason in us, but we have reason in us too. If the universe has vast stretches of darkness in it, it also has small areas of light—and these are what give it significance.

And human life, if it has significance, is this not where it finds it—in these areas of light, of reason, of order? A man strikes a match and holds it up before him and presses ahead while the light lasts.

So he makes his way a little further through the dark. And often he leaves footprints for the rest of us to follow, so that little by little the unknown way becomes the known.

A story of growth

The story of life is a story of growth.

Life makes sense in the truest sense of life—life is alive and grows.

The astronomers, the geologists, the biologists tell us that in the beginning there was merely amorphous stuff, shapeless drifting clouds in space. The stuff formed into fireballs, and in the fireball we call earth the stuff formed into seas and land. After a long time, bacteria and algae swarmed in the seas.

But the bacteria and algae did not remain bacteria and algae. The bacteria and algae did not go back into shapeless stuff again. They grew.

They became ever more complex, took ever more various shapes, grew ever more alive.

How strange that in a meaningless world that which was shapeless stuff should have become such complex and beautiful shapes as sharks, moths, trees, birds, toadstools, and human beings! Why should it not have gone the other way? Would it not be reasonable to have expected it to?

In a meaningless world, would we not think to see life crumble into death; intelligence molder into stupidity; love coarsen into brutality?

But this is not the way the world went at all. It went in the opposite direction.

Death became life, and life became yet more livingly alive. Stupidity became intelligence, and intelligence became the power to see and feel and reason and reach beyond. Brutality became love, and love became the power to sacrifice self-interest, to risk life itself to save another—sometimes even a stranger.

And humankind—what has been our story?

Our story has been the story of growth, only growth.

A best-seller in our day has been *Lord of the Flies*. In this book some English schoolboys are marooned on an island and quickly degenerate into vicious brutes.

"Aha!" cry the cynical. "See how wicked human beings would be if they only had a chance!"

But we have had a chance.

The human condition is exactly that of the boys on the island in the story.

About a million years ago, the human race found itself alone on this island the earth—and human history is the story of what it has done on its island ever since.

Far from sinking from a civilized state to a savage one, we lifted ourselves from a savage state to a civilized one. Instead of proper English schoolboys turning into savages, savages have turned into proper English schoolboys.

To those scribes who like to say of Man, "He hath the Lord of the Flies," I can only reply in the words of the Son of Man, "How can Satan cast out Satan?"

For no one made human beings better. They grew better because it is their nature to grow better. They have in them the tendency not to fall into bestiality, but to rise into humanity.

The cunning brute, living only to eat and reproduce and sleep, clawing a hard life hard-heartedly from a hard earth, has become intelligent Man, Homo sapiens, even gentle Man!

Probably in most of us the ancient brute still lurks in a not-too-distant cave. We are still too selfish and self-centered. We are still too indifferent to the good of others so long as our own needs are met. We are still too capable of cruelty. But human history has been the story of the substitution of kindness for cruelty, of law for force, of order for license, of responsibility for indifference. Human history has been the story of the pursuit of excellence and knowledge and peace and emancipation from pain and oppression for all.

Human history has been the story of the slow decrease in the number of cruel, ignorant, aggressive, self-centered people, and of the slow increase in the number of those who are kinder, more just, more charitable, more concerned for the welfare of others.

We see more intelligence in the world today than has ever been seen before. We see more concern for justice. We see more concern for others.

How far have we grown?

History is change.

More than change, history is growth.

How far have we grown?

Twenty-five thousand years ago, if you had encountered the gentlest person alive, you would have fled in terror as from a monster. And you would have been wise to flee, for that person would have had only one interest in you—to devour you.

Four thousand years ago, the Hebrews conquered Canaan. When they took a city, they slew every inhabitant—man, woman, and child.

Two thousand years ago, Rome conquered Carthage. They tore down the city, strewed salt where it had been, executed all the men, and sold the women and children as slaves.

How different the conquest of Japan by the United States in our own time!

Knowledge, too, has made steady growth.

There is a great deal of ignorance today. But compare it with the ignorance of twenty-five thousand years ago. Or even with the ignorance of two thousand years ago or two hundred years ago.

In the Golden Age of Greece and Rome, most people were illiterate slaves. In a half-dozen cities, a handful of people—in all not more than a few thousand—exchanged ideas, studied, and wrote.

We have been taught to think that knowledge disappeared when Greece and Rome disappeared. The fact is there were more centers of learning and more educated people in the so-called Dark Ages than in the time of Pericles. In our own time, of course, there has been an explosion of learning.

Hitlers still squirm their way into power—but for every Hitler there are a hundred heads of state trying to be decent, honest, and just. When a Hitler appears, most of the world stands aghast and ashamed.

Instead of pointing to the occasional Hitler and saying, "How wicked human beings are!" why do we not point to the heroism and self-sacrifice that go on around us every day and say, "How good human beings are!"

Looking backward at our history, we see winters as well as springs, but always the tree has put forth leaf and grown again.

And the tree is life; the tree is knowledge; the tree is love.

And the tree is still alive. The tree is still growing.

During World War II, a Norwegian girl was taken before a Nazi commander because she had been sharing her bread with Russian prisoners.

"But I was taught to be kind to my fellowmen," said the girl.

"But have we not taught you these are not men but beasts?"

"I was taught," said the girl, "to be kind to beasts."

How far have we come!

Evolution did not stop

How far have we come? And how far are we going?

Evolution is not something that happened.

Evolution is going on now.

Evolution did not stop with the fossils.

Evolution did not stop with the appearance of Homo sapiens.

Modern Man is not a final product. Modern Man is an evolving product.

Our generation is not the same as that of our grandparents. Our grandchildren's generation will not be the same as ours.

How will they be different?

We are too close to see—but they will be different.

Imagine a pine forest. In the pine forest a hickory tree sprouts. After a hundred years there are a dozen hickory trees. After a thousand years there are thousands of hickory trees. After several thousand years there are more hickory trees than pine trees. Then in the hickory forest, where a few pine trees still grow, an elm tree sprouts. After a hundred years there are a dozen elm trees. And so it goes, ad infinitum.

Nature does not have to hurry; she has aeons of time and most of the time she takes it. But she never stands still.

Perhaps at this very moment an individual is being born with some slightly different mental or emotional tendency. Perhaps you were born with some slightly different trait that makes you more vital, that makes you stronger or quicker or hardier or more attractive or more long-lived.

Today there is one such individual. But the way the human race is going, a hundred years from now there will be a hundred human beings with such a trait. A thousand years from now there will be many more. Come back twenty-five thousand years from now and you will find few human beings who do not have such a trait.

Twenty-five thousand years ago, the first impulse of most of the human beings you would have encountered would have been to kill you if they could.

Today the first impulse of most human beings is a friendly one.

There are still truculent, unfriendly human beings. But these are fewer than they were twenty-five thousand years ago, five thousand years ago, five hundred years ago. Five hundred years from now they will be fewer yet. Five thousand years from now they may have become so rare that the rest of us will look at them with astonishment and treat them with tender care as curious carryovers from a bygone age.

The human being is the first mental animal. Until now life's concern has been with physical growth. Things have evolved from simpler to more complex, more adaptable forms. And life will never cease to shape new shapes in infinite variety on every plane and level of existence. This is its nature.

But human beings are traveling a new road. We may be evolving with little or no outward sign of change. For we may be evolving in mind. We may be evolving in spirit. This is where the great growth is going to take place for human beings.

A hundred thousand years from now men and women may look not too unlike what they do now, yet be changed in every fiber of their being.

It may even be that we may gain control of our own

evolution and determine for ourselves what direction we will take.

If we do, we may at first do foolish and unpleasant things to ourselves and one another. But not for long. For the spirit in us that brought us this far—that turned savage beasts into sometime saints—can be trusted to keep us on our way.

If the nightmares of Huxley's *Brave New World* or Orwell's *1984* should become reality, if we managed to turn earth into a concentration camp where we drugged and brainwashed one another into brutal automatons, even this would not last for long.

Soon—oh, very soon, much sooner than we think—the human spirit would assert itself and the human race would rise and shake its own vermin from its back.

Because it is our nature not to remain brute.

We cannot violate our nature for long. We did not settle for brutality, and we never will. We will never settle for less than the realization of the highest and best that is in us.

Looking backward, looking forward

Human history is the history of growth.

It has been a long journey.

Looking backward, we may observe meanders where the river seemed to turn back on itself. But always when we look farther on, it becomes evident that the river did not turn back, it swept on nearer to the sea.

Looking backward as far as we can see, we see only growth.

The shapeless takes shape; the inanimate becomes animate; the one-celled becomes many-celled; the many-celled becomes plants and animals; the animals become human beings, beings whose highest concerns are not of the flesh but of the mind. The unconscious becomes conscious; the simple conscious becomes self-conscious; the self-conscious becomes selflessly conscious!

Human beings are no more the end of the journey than the dinosaur was. It is ours to carry the torch of life along the path, but we, too, will pass it on to stronger runners. Man will be more than Man.

Earth lives and will die. Even the sun will go out at last. At last even the galaxy.

But there will be other earths and suns, other galaxies. There will be other worlds.

There will be worlds beyond galaxies, beyond space, beyond dimension, beyond conceiving, beyond imagining.

And through them all the river of life will run—broad, splendid, shining, deep, irresistible, growing—rolling in a glorious torrent toward that infinite, eternal sea, where all waters have their rise and their returning.

What is this world?

What is this world?

What are you?

What brought the world into being? Is it a vast machine? Is it an accident?

Has the world always been here? Or did something make it—or Somebody?

Is it all just the result of natural processes—and what does that mean?

Have you never asked such questions?

For answers, to whom have you turned—to scientists, to philosophers, to religious revelation? I say you can answer these questions for yourself.

Do not take my answers—or anyone else's. All of us—the most bemedaled of us, the most bemitered, the most bemantled with university degrees—we are all theorizing or pontificating.

Find your answers for yourself.

How?

Look for them. Look at yourself. Look at the world around you.

Truth is not secret or hidden, to be ferreted out only with microscopes and telescopes and computers.

Truth reveals itself to all of us all the time.

Truth reveals itself to everyone—even to everything.

Truth is not something God has reserved for the learned only. Truth is not something God has kept from us until we could invent machines to track it down.

I believe my cat has as much access to truth as I do—and finds it too. Only he expresses it in cat terms and relates it to cat needs. I believe amoebas find truth. They express it in amoeba terms, that is all.

Truth is constantly, persistently, insistently, overwhelmingly seeking to express itself, seeking to give itself to us.

It presents itself before us in ten thousand forms and faces; it speaks to us in tongues; dances under our fingers; undulates under our feet; presses itself against us; flings itself over us; coils itself around us. "Take me. Know me. Experience me," truth cries.

It burns in our flesh. It wings through our thoughts. It

prods us with visions and dreams.

It speaks from every atom of our world and every moment of our life.

Everything is trying to tell us what it is.

Everything is trying to tell us what we are.

Truth is a diamond with ten thousand facets, and life would have you look through them all.

So I say to you, look at yourself. Look at the world around you.

You do not even have to look deep. Look at the surface of things. That is enough.

Go to the window and look. What do you see?

Sky, clouds, trees, grass, buildings, streets, living creatures darting here and there—colors, shapes more various than any you can see in a kaleidoscope, all changing all the time, grouping, regrouping, never twice the same.

One thing the briefest look will tell you: The mechanists-behaviorists-materialists-naturalists—whatever they may call themselves who call the world and themselves a machine—these are wrong.

They are as wrong as human beings can be wrong. And this—because they are not machines—is very, very wrong.

Whatever the world came out of, this Whatever is alive.

Whatever It Is that made the world, the word that describes Him worst is *machine*. I say Him because the word I like best is *God* and I learned to think of God as Him.

I cannot believe you can look out a window and think you are looking at a machine—or that it came out of a machine.

What you see out there is as unlike machinery as anyone can conceive. If there is anything it does not make you think of, it is gears, wheels, pulleys, belts, motors, electrical circuits, computers, and mills stamping out finished products at a fixed and steady rate, over and over, over and over.

The nature of a machine is that it repeats itself. Set it in operation and it will everlastingly—or until it breaks down—stamp out exactly, repeatedly whatever it is set to stamp out.

What you see out there never repeats itself. This is one thing it does not do—repeat itself.

Look.

Look away.

Look again.

Everything you are looking at has already changed.

What you see out there changes as the changing wind—blows here, there, everywhere. Whatever It Is that made it has never made two moments alike. Not two snowflakes. Not two thumbprints.

Out there is a bird. It perches on a bough, sings, leaps up, perches on another bough, flutters down to peck at a seed, preens, cocks its head, flies up to a bough again, flies away. It may or may not fly back. Another bird may, after a while. And again it may not.

Out there are bees buzzing in the clover, sipping this blossom, spurning that, wallowing in golden pollen, zooming upward, gliding downward, banking, diving, hovering, lurching, flying off, returning.

Out there is a tree.

Nothing stands for life more than a tree; nothing is a better symbol of the world.

A tree grows down into the earth; a tree grows up into the sky. It sends out roots and branches everywhere, an almost inconceivable network of them, up, down, out, in, horizontally, vertically, crisscrossing, overlapping, circling, no two alike, almost a pattern of disorder, of random, irregular, haphazard growth, of absence of design—yet nothing is more a part of nature's order than a tree.

Tranquil, breathing, resting, growing, responding effortlessly to the ebb and surge of the seasons, a tree is life and a perfect expression of life.

Whatever It Is that made this tree of life is alive.

When you think about the world around you, what thoughts come to your mind?

You know that you are under law. Cause and effect are at work in your life. You know that many of the things that happen to you are determined by things that have gone before. Certainly you cannot look out at the world without having a sense of order.

But you cannot look out without having a sense of disorder too. You cannot think of yourself without feeling that you are free. Just as good a term as cause and effect, to describe why things happen as they happen to happen, is freedom.

One time I heard a chemist say that in every chemical reaction there comes a moment when things could just as easily go one way as the other—only they do not choose to.

The world is an orderly world. It is run by laws. But it is also a random world, altogether original, various, unpredictable, perpetually bringing off surprises, constantly delighting in its own inventive play.

The world is not a machine. It is a world alive. And Whatever It Is that made it is alive.

Purpose and destination

Whatever It Is that made this world made it for a purpose. The world is not just something that happened. Life is not just something that happened. You are not just something that happened.

I do not believe there have ever been human beings who felt they had no purpose for being. We may lose sight of our purpose. We may despair of achieving it. But lose the feeling that we have some purpose? Never. Even when we cry out, "Life seems to have lost its purpose!" our purpose is to find one.

All our life we are impelled by purposes—some lofty and great, some miserable and small.

Living beings are impelled by purposes. Whenever I think of things in terms of life or in terms of mind, I have to think in terms of purposes. Whenever I think, I am in a world of purpose.

This is another reason for believing we are not machines— or parts of a machine. Machines operate by causes, not from purposes.

When I look at the world from outside in, I see causes. But when I look from inside out, I see purposes. Causes work on matter. Purposes work in minds. Cause is a force pushing out of the past; purpose is an idea guiding into the future. Purpose is the sign of mind.

Is it spring because the sun crossed the equator? Or did the sun cross the equator because Whatever It Is that made the world loves spring, loves loveliness, loves life, loves change, loves growing things?

In a world of machines, every event is the consequence of

a previous event which it follows by necessity. The belt moved because the wheel turned because the gears meshed because the lever was pressed. And each of these events—unless there is a breakdown—has inevitably to follow the one that preceded it; there can be no alteration of this order.

But in a world of mind the opposite is true. I start to throw the ball to my teammate because I want him to pass to my other teammate because the latter can dribble down underneath the basket and score a goal. But at the last moment I see that my pass may be blocked, so I whirl, dribble, pass to a third teammate, dart under the goal myself to receive the ball back from him, and shoot.

What a world of difference we see here.

The machine must automatically run through its processes to carry out the designs of its designer. But I—I am the designer!

I choose between courses of action and follow this one instead of that one because my purpose is to reach a certain goal.

I was not cast out to sea, pushed on by wind and wave to drift wherever they may blow me. I set out for a port.

No blind sequence of events sweeping out of the past determines my action.

I have a destination!

And this world has a destination.

I may not know where it is going, but it is going there. And this I do know: Whatever the destination is, it is something so great and good that great and good are not great and good enough names for it.

You can call it heaven if you want to. Or perfection. Or unity with God.

All I know is that when you get there, it will be a starting point. Not just a port of call, but also a port of embarkation.

Whatever It Is is mind

Where there is purpose, there is Mind.

Whatever It Is that made the world, It is Mind. Mind is a feeble word for It, but Mind is the least It can be called. It made you—and you are Mind.

Creative Mind dreamed forth this world of forms and movement, light and thought, and wrapped it in space and cradled it in time.

Without Mind, there is meaningless activity.

With Mind, nothing is meaningless. Mind gives meaning to everything. This is almost the definition of Mind: the presence of meaning. We know Mind is present because meaning is present.

The world is like music—small, meaningless marks strung across a set of horizontal lines and spaces until the musician comes. But when the musician looks at the cryptic marks, he hears a concord of sweet sounds.

Mind is the Musician.

Without Mind there are only meaningless electrons whirling in whateverness. Not even so much as that, for it is Mind that identifies the meaningless whateverness and cries out, "Electrons!"

Only in Mind do the electrons take shape and form patterns—dance, sing, fly, flow, grow, and live; become hills and rivers, fields and woods, the sun and the stars, men and women, you and me. Only in Mind does the whateverness become a world.

The moment Mind appears, the world has meaning, for Mind gives it meaning. Mind says, "World!"

You cannot conceive of a world without Mind, for without Mind you cannot conceive.

Mind gives meaning. Mind is meaning. Without Mind, how shall I even think, "It is meaningless"?

Whatever It Is loves beauty

Whatever It Is that made the world loves beauty. It had to make the sun, perhaps–but not sunsets. It needed rain—but not rainbows. The world would run smoothly without butter-flies or roses or redbirds—it would just not be so beautiful.

Go out under the night sky and look at the stars that litter the floor of heaven like falling leaves. Go out in the autumn wood and look at the leaves that litter the forest floor like falling stars. Go look at the flowering trees of spring. Go walk through falling snow. Something is at work here that loves beauty. Can you look at the world around you and believe anything else?

I realize that the world is beautiful because I find it so. It is I who love the form and sound of the waves that break on the beach; it is I who love the shape of trees, the song of a summer stream, the flight of birds.

But that I have a sense of the beautiful is no less an indica-tion of what the world is like than that beauty is there to be sensed.

For I see ugliness too. And is this not even more remark-able? If beauty were simply my way of looking at things, my way of apprehending what is, why should I see anything else?

Above all, why should I see beauty in a storm or a deadly

flower or the face of my enemy?

A machine make honeybees, hummingbirds, petunias? I do not believe it.

O You who made stars, dust, and me

If you want to know what Whatever It Is that made the world is like, look at yourself.

What are you like?

Full of hopes, fears, desires, ambitions, serenity, angers, disappointments, elation, thoughts, dreams, longings, memories; capable of love, capable of selflessness.

Whatever It Is that made the world certainly is not less than you are. It may be more—much more—but it is not less.

Think for a moment about yourself.

Are you a machine?

You behaviorist-mechanists, do you feel like machines?

I wonder if the loudest behaviorist-mechanist alive has ever for a single moment felt that he was a machine? He only theorizes about it. He works it out on graphs, not in his blood and bone and breath. He can think, "We are machines," but he cannot live like one.

What kind of machine is this that if you make four billion of them displays four billion kinds of behavior?

What kind of machine is this that can sacrifice, renounce, spurn punishment and reward, break precedents, defy rules, find new ways of operating, renew itself, repair itself, destroy itself, or rise beyond itself?

How many times these human-machines have given up bread for poetry, riches for love, idle ease for perilous adventure.

How many times, out of the hope of helping others, these machines have given up their own hope even of life.

How many times they have walked into the black and icy void of the unknown, uncertain they will ever find their way back out again—just to find out what is there.

Born to be hunters, with teeth to rend and juices to digest the flesh of other creatures, they can out of pity become vegetarians.

Starving and in rags, they can out of pride spurn the coin cast at them in scorn.

Frightened, without hope of succor, tortured, facing death, they can out of devotion to truth refuse to betray what they believe.

Tormented and hung up to die, at least one of them could out of love pray for forgiveness for those who tormented Him.

Look at yourself—at your best.

What was the noblest moment of your life?

What is the most inspired insight you have ever had?

What is the bravest act you have ever done?

What is the most selfless gift you have ever given?

What is the most sublime joy you have ever experienced?

Have you never hoped and striven to do impossible things?

Have you never gone beyond yourself?

Have you never touched powers you would not have believed you had?

Have you never dreamed of yourself as something more than yourself? What were you then?

For then, when you soared beyond yourself in your noblest dream, in your noblest hope, in your noblest thought, in your noblest deed, in your noblest moment—then you caught a glimpse of what That One is like who made you and your world.

For you are made in the image of That One, and at your heart's core—in your essence if not in your existence—you are one with That One.

What is That One that you are one with?

I can say Intelligence.

I can say Love.

I can say Spirit.

I can say Creative Joy.

They are all inadequate words.

I look up at the stars—every star a world—and stars past counting—worlds and worlds and worlds of stars past even my power to imagine.

I look down at the ground—every grain of dust a world— shall I try to count the countless grains of dust?

O You who made stars, dust, and me who am both dust and stars, Lord of the infinitesimal and the infinite, of in and out, of space and thought; I have not mounted even the first step of Your throne.

Yet I think I have glimpsed Your face when I look at the face of my brothers and sisters. I think I have touched Your hand when I touch the green leaves of spring.

I do not know all You are, for whatever I imagine You to be, You are yet more. But I know somewhat that You are.

You are life. You are mind. You are the love of beauty. You

are God. You are the divinity that I feel stirring even within myself.

world of atoms——world of faith

TWO

A streak of materialism

Most of us have a strong streak of materialism in us. Perhaps it would be more precise to say we are realists; we all believe that the world our senses reveal to us is the real world, and that anything we cannot see, hear, touch, taste, or smell has not as much reality as what we can.

We all say of some event, "It really happened," or "It was only in his mind."

We say of a stone, "It is real." We say of a dream, "It was only a dream."

Most of us most of the time know the difference between an actual stone and an imagined stone—or do we?

When we say about some experience we are having, "This is a thought," it never seems as real to us as when we say, "This is a thing."

We lay hold of thoughts with our sense; we lay hold of things with our senses.

But what are sense and senses?

Both sense and senses are powers of the mind. They are aspects of mind. They are mind. Whether it is with our sense or our senses that we lay hold of thoughts or things, we are laying hold of them with our mind. Different aspects of mind, but mind. This is an important notion to grasp.

Do you think you can lay hold of things with your hands? Certainly you do. But when you say you lay hold of things with your hands, what do you mean? You mean that you touch them. But touch is a sense. You mean that you grasp them. But that is to say you have a sense of weight and shape.

We lay hold of thoughts with our mind—our thinking faculty. We lay hold of things with our mind—our sensing, perceiving faculty.

What we lay hold of with our senses seems more real to us than what we lay hold of with our thoughts alone. Most of the time, at least. Sometimes, however, we have a hard time telling thought from thing; we think we have hold of something with our senses, but it turns out to be only in our thought, as with a mirage or a hallucination. Sometimes our thought has to correct what our senses tell us, as when two parallel lines, like railroad tracks, seem to run together to our sight, but we know they do not. Or a stick we thrust into the water seems to bend, but we know it is still straight.

Nevertheless, in spite of our occasional confusion, most of us most of the time feel that what we lay hold of with our senses is more real than what we lay hold of only in our thought.

Especially when several of us agree that we are tasting, smelling, hearing, seeing, and feeling something, we say of it, "It is really there." And "there" has a special meaning that is hard to define, but one we all understand.

And the more senses we can lay hold of anything with, the more real it seems. Thus, stones seem more real than air—until we cannot lay hold of the air. Then how quickly air becomes the only real thing!

Likewise, to most of us food seems more real than love. But I wonder, if we should lose love, would it be food or love that would seem more real then? And peace of mind is just a state of mind, is it not? But if we lose it, does any orderly arrangement of things in the world outside count for as much?

To return to stones and air, the materialists, of course, consider air to be one of the real things. Solids, liquids, gases—these are all equally real, they would say. They would even admit energy into their category; light, heat, electricity—these are real. So they have gotten back to Aristotle's earth, water, air, and fire; the great Greek taught that everything could be grouped into these four classes. But the modern materialists do not stop with this.

Reality, according to the physicists, consists mostly of empty space. In this empty space move invisible particles that may not even be particles; for sometimes they seem more like energy than matter. At any rate, these unimaginably tiny particles move at vast distances relative to one another. And anything you say about them and their motion—by the principle of indeterminacy—is not true all the time.

This is the kind of reality that modern science has presented to us.

Is it really easier to accept than the notion, say, that what is there is what our mind tells us is there?

I do not think that most of us have paused to consider how far the scientists—whom we think of as hardheaded realists and materialists—have taken us from what we ordinarily, and from day to day, think reality, materiality, or actuality is.

Just as in the Middle Ages we accepted what the priests told us was real, so now we have transferred the authority we gave them to the scientists, our new priesthood. We are content to accept whatever they tell us is real because what they tell us has been working. It lights and heats and cools our houses, heals our bodies, transports us around the earth and into space, and even on occasion—with an atomic explosion—into the next world. No, I am sorry. I should not put it that way, because many of these new priests in the temple of science tell us there is no next world.

They have proved that natural man's real world of stones, rivers, air, and fields of daisies—the world we live in—is only an appearance, only the way our senses report to us on what is really there.

They have substituted for this the physicists' real world of empty space, particles, waves, and motion. "This is what is really there," they say.

And every day they make startling new discoveries as to what is really real. "Surprises come often," they say.

The farther they penetrate into the woods, the deeper the woods become. The more they find out, the less they know with certainty.

But this is certain: The more they find out, the less like what we thought was real reality becomes.

Reality is not the sticks and stones we thought it was, but uncertain and changing clouds of force moving in emptiness.

The materialists have followed the path of materiality as far and as hard as they could.

And where has it come out?

Some two or three thousand years ago the Hindus and Buddhists were talking about reality. They, too, abandoned the notion that the appearance of things—the sticks and stones—is really real.

And they came up with notions that they named *Brahma, nirvana,* and, the most interesting name of all, *sunyata,* or "the void." Reality, they said, is void of attributes.

They thought of reality as an impenetrable, deep, and changing ocean, carrying on its surface the tossing momentary waves that are the shapes and ideas we sense and conceive.

They did not use scientific language, of course. They used mystical terms. But following the path of mysticism as far

44

and as hard as they could, they arrived at concepts almost exactly like those that the scientist-materialists of our time have arrived at, following the path of materialism.

The mystics went in; the scientists have gone out. Can it be that in and out are just two directions from which to view one reality?

Apparently, if you go far enough in either direction, you arrive at the same idea of what reality is.

A big word often used today to describe reality is *continuum*. Another word is *field*.

Would you like to get a notion of what the physicists (and the mystics) believe to be reality?

Think of a field. It has to stretch as far as you can see, edgeless as a Kansas prairie. It is full of daisies. See them growing and blowing in the wind.

Now take away all the daisies.

Now take away all the particles of soil.

What do you have left?

There is just— —.

But it immediately fills again with particles of soil and with daisies—or with any and all of the infinitely various, infinitely changing forms that the field may grow into.

What is really real?

Philosophers have argued about reality from the beginning of philosophy, which is to say ever since human beings have been human.

They have chewed it to rags and pretty well proved that you can find reason to believe almost anything you want to believe.

There is no more reason for believing that reality is things than that it is thought—perhaps a lot less.

What is a thing?

As you can see from the last chapter, it is not easy to say.

When modern science began its investigation of things, certain qualities of things seemed much more real to them than other qualities. These qualities were those that they could weigh and measure with instruments in laboratories. They were qualities that seemed independent of mind. For instance, the frequency and wavelength of light.

Qualities like the color the lightwave took—magenta lilac, for instance—seemed to depend on mind, and might even vary from observer to observer, so these did not seem so really real.

But about two hundred fifty years ago, an English bishop named Berkeley saw that frequency, wavelength, and the like are just as much ways in which the mind sees things as is color.

The atomic weight of the metal in a golden trumpet is just as much a concept of mind as is the sound the trumpet makes when it is blown.

Berkeley advanced the notion that there is nothing but mind and the ideas in it. Reality, he taught, is mind. There is no matter; matter is an idea in your mind, and so are all its qualities, whether they are measurements made in a laboratory and marked down in ohms, miles per hour, pounds, or centimeters; or whether they are colors, sounds, and theories. Everything is an idea in your mind; mind and its ideas are all there is.

Samuel Johnson, the irascible old dictionary maker, disposed of this notion, he thought, by kicking a stone. "That," he said to Boswell, rubbing his toe, "is my answer to Berkeley."

We all feel a little like Johnson, but, of course, all he had done was add to Berkeley's proof. Not only was the stone a gray, round object to his sight and a hard, round object to his touch, but it was now also a pain that he felt—and not even Johnson would have maintained that pain was not in his mind (although most of us are such materialists that we differentiate even among pains; there are real and imaginary pains, we say).

If, however, we forget pains and toes and agree with the physicists that the stone is really minute particles whirling in space in such a way that our senses report these whirling particles to us as a gray, round object we call a stone, we simply have substituted many minute, invisible, speeding particles for a single, gray, round, hard object.

The particles, even more than the single object, exist in our mind. For no one has ever seen the particles that the atomic theory tells us a stone is composed of. Atoms are a theory advanced to explain certain facts that we observe about the way things act.

Cloud chambers, X-ray machines, cyclotrons, and other devices offer evidence that such particles exist, but the particles themselves—if they do exist—are too small to be observed, even with the most powerful instruments we have devised.

The atomic theory explains the facts we have observed better than any previous explanation. So we believe in atoms.

But atoms themselves—let alone electrons, the even smaller particles of which atoms are supposed to be composed—have never been seen.

One of these days, someone may come up with a better explanation than the atomic theory offers of why things act the way they act, just as the atomic theory supplanted earlier theories.

So it was with Berkeley. A young Scot named Hume read what Berkeley had written and decided that the good bishop had not gone far enough in his analysis of what is real. Berkeley's *mind*, wrote Hume, is just a notion too. Mind is no more real than matter; in reality there is nothing but thought following thought from moment to moment in the—he did not use the Buddhists' word *void*, but he could have.

Hume altered our notion of reality. He left of it nothing except tossing, momentary waves—of an ocean that was not there!—until a German philosopher named Kant came along and, in one of the most hard-to-understand books ever written, advanced the notion that there is a real world—that is, a world that exists independent of our mind, of our knowledge of it, and of our thoughts. But it's a world we can only experience with our mind, so we can never know for certain what it really is, but only know it as our mind reveals it to us. We must see it through the window of our mind.

The world is a garden, but for you and me it is a garden as seen from one window, one vantage point—the window of our mind. So it has to look like what I can see from that window. If I could see the world from a different vantage point, I might describe it to you in very different terms.

Truth is a view from a window. What window are you looking through?

Those in the East—the sages of Hinduism and Buddhism—had reached similar conclusions thousands of years before, although they used different language from Berkeley's or Hume's or Kant's to describe their thoughts.

You probably remember from your childhood the famous fable of the blind men and the elephant.

Some blind men wished to know what an elephant was like, so they examined one. "The elephant is like a tree," said the first, who had taken hold of its leg. "The elephant is like a wall," said the second, who had felt its side. "The elephant is like a fan," said the third, who had grasped its ear. "The elephant is like a snake," said the fourth, who had laid hold of its trunk. "The elephant is like a rope," said the fifth, who had taken hold of its tail. "The elephant is like a spear," said the sixth, who had slid his hands along its tusk. So the blind men fell to disputing among themselves.

Let us leave the blind men and go back and pick up the stone again.

We say that the stone is gray, round, hard.

Are these qualities in the stone?

If we were thoroughgoing materialists, we would have to say so. But if we were thoroughgoing materialists, we would have to say also that the stone is really a collection of atoms. What we really have picked up—what is really there—is atoms.

But are atoms gray?

Are atoms round?

Are atoms hard?

Atoms have never been seen. They have never been felt by anyone's hand. So it is impossible to say what they are like.

Still, it is questionable that they are gray or round or hard. According to the theory, they are probably none of these. We can make the stone glow. We can crush it. We can liquefy and gasify it. The atoms are still there, but the grayness, roundness, hardness have vanished.

Grayness, roundness, hardness, then, are not qualities of the atoms—if there are atoms.

Where, then, do they exist?

There is only one place left where they can exist.

That is in my mind.

They are my mind's way of describing what it experiences when it comes in contact with what I call a stone.

As I have said, we all have a strong tendency to accept as real the stone that our senses tell us is there.

But in our age we have come to accept as even more really real the stone that scientific theory tells us is there!

The real stone—that is, if we have been intellectually indoctrinated in scientific theory and impressed enough by scientific achievement, as I have been and probably you have been too—is not the stone we see and handle, but the stone as it is to our scales, calipers, chemical tests, microscopes— and scientific theories! This is reason's stone—the stone of sense, not senses!

We have come to believe that scientific theory reveals to us a reality of a deeper and more real sort than just our senses reveal to us.

If I ask you, "What is the earth?" do you not immediately think of a spinning ball, a perfect sphere whirling in space which is a perfect, three-dimensional medium, where each dimension is at right angles to the others?

But have you ever seen such an earth? Indeed, if the astronomers and geophysicists are right, earth is not a per- fect sphere, but a somewhat irregular, pear-shaped thing. And space may be very unlike this mathematical construct we make it in our mind.

The point is that when we think of reality, we may not be thinking what we thoughtlessly think we are thinking at all.

We may be thinking of a reality that exists only in a theory—and not even the hardest-headed materialist would claim that a theory exists anywhere outside of mind.

Most of us probably accept the world that our senses

reveal to us as real; at the same time we accept as real the world that scientific theory has revealed to us. And we do this without questioning that these are very different worlds.

But they are very different worlds. The stone of whirling atoms and the perfect spinning earth are not anything we see; they are what we conceive earth and stone to be in theory.

I am not trying to prove that the theory is wrong. For the present it is right. Because it is all we need to know. Sooner or later some bright scientist will come along and prove that it is wrong, for he will find some things that cannot be explained by the atomic theory.

I am not trying to prove that things are this or that; it is all right with me if you believe that what your senses reveal is real, or if you believe that what your sense (in our day, scientific theory) reveals is real.

What I am trying to do is to get you to think about what you do believe to be real. I am trying to get you to use your senses and your sense and take a look at the world around you.

When you think of the real, what do you think of?

What is reality?

The modern materialist would have us believe that all there is is a flow of energy in emptiness. But if this is so, it is obvious that we experience it as forms and thoughts. For none of us have ever experienced a flow of energy in emptiness; the very phrase is such an abstract concept in our mind that it takes a very good mind to grasp what it means.

Berkeley and Hume taught that reality is merely the flow of sensations, perceptions, and concepts that pass through our mind—that is, of our ideas.

Kant and the Eastern mystics believe that reality is

essentially unknowable except in those terms in which our mind (because of its own structure) experiences it.

But whether it is energy or thought or unknowable except as mind knows it, one thing is certain: reality is what we make of it in mind.

Let us then look to what is in our mind; for whatever is, this is true about it—whether we are mystics or materialists, physicists or metaphysicists—we can handle it only with our mind.

Faith makes the difference

A man named Jesus lived two thousand years ago. He made many claims about Himself and about us; He taught about life and how we should live.

But over and over this man indicated that there are two important factors on which our life depends. There are two factors that determine what every person's life is like.

One factor is desire.

The other factor is faith.

Jesus taught this clearly and simply. He taught this many, many times.

"Ask," He said. "Ask, and it will be given you."

And even more often He said, "Believe."

"Only believe." "Your faith has made you well."

"If you have faith as a grain of mustard seed, you will say to this mountain, 'Move . . .' and it will move."

"All things are possible to him who believes."

I have never counted all the places in the Bible where Jesus said that you get what you desire and what you believe in.

These are, of course, tremendous and extraordinary teachings. At first thought they seem unreasonable.

What we desire we get?

What we have faith in comes to pass?

Hard to believe!

But the man who believed and taught these teachings influenced and altered life on this earth more than any other person who has ever lived.

Can these be true teachings?

Let us look at them.

What is faith?

We get to thinking that faith is something religious people have, but I think Jesus was using the word in a much broader sense, for it has a broader sense.

Is not faith what we think and feel to be true?

Your faith is what you think and feel to be true.

My faith is what I think and feel to be true.

What we think and feel to be true! Reflect on this for a moment. Is this not what we live by? And when what we think and feel to be true changes, is it possible for our life to go on the same?

And desire! Does desire not bend and shape what we think and feel to be true? So is it not always bending and shaping our life in the direction it is taking?

Everyone has faith. That is, we think and feel certain things to be true.

Your faith is not what you say you believe.

Your faith is not what you speculate to be true.

Your faith is what you believe in the inmost fibers of your being, in the deep core of yourself. Your faith is what you believe so deeply that you may not even know you believe it; it is simply what you base your life on.

With some of your faith—probably a great deal of it—you were born; it is your heritage as a human being.

Some of your faith you absorbed unconsciously from the way of life that went on around you as an infant. People said and did things that gave you a view of life which you accepted without ever knowing what you were doing and without knowing there might be another view.

Some of your faith you were taught—by your parents, by the children you played with, by the school you went to, and by the community you grew up in.

Your faith is your basic beliefs, the beliefs you live by, what you feel to be true, what you think to be true. Some of it you are aware of; you know you are a Catholic or a Protestant or a Jew, a Democrat or a Republican or a Communist. You know whether you believe in God or not, whether you believe in Jesus Christ or not. These are a few of the thousands of beliefs you have and know that you have.

But a great deal of your faith—perhaps most of what you believe most deeply, what you live by and are ruled by and even will die for—a great deal of it you are not aware of. Certainly you have never put it into words and would have a hard time doing so.

But your faith—expressed and unexpressed—is what makes you you.

If you are an American, for instance, you have a set of beliefs. You are unaware of many of them, but you have them just because you are an American.

They are what make you different from other people.

All of us have faith. What is important is what our faith is in. We live by our faith, whether we know it or not, and what we believe determines our lives.

It matters a great deal whether you think and feel that life is a meaningless accident or that life is meaningful and purposeful.

It matters a great deal whether you think and feel that there is a God or not.

And it matters as much what you believe God to be.

Do you believe that God lives in a distant heaven or that God is in your heart and instantly available?

Do you believe that God is a superperson on a throne or that God is the ruling order and principle of being, everywhere at hand, always at work?

Do you believe that God is He—or She?

Do you believe that God is a stern judge who thrusts people into eternal damnation or that God is the power of love working to bring all things to perfection?

Do you believe that God made human beings and their world evil or that God made them good?

What do you believe you are?

A worm of the dust or a child of God? A chemical accident in a blind world of haphazard energies, or a spiritual being with a divine purpose?

Do you believe that you were made to suffer and die, or made for life and life abundant, for health, for love, for joy, for perfection?

It makes a great deal of difference what you believe. Jesus said it makes all the difference. "According to your faith," He taught, it shall be.

This man clearly did not believe that the important things in this world are energy and atoms. He indicated that what is important is what you believe and desire.

What you think and feel and want to be true—this determines what your life is like.

Man's three-sided nature

Plato and Aristotle and the greatest thinkers of ancient times all taught that we human beings have a three-sided nature. We are mind, spirit, and will, they said, or thought, feeling, and desire. Modern psychologists have not improved on this analysis.

What do you think, feel, and want to be true? This—what you are in consciousness—is what matters.

But remember, it is not what you say you think, what you say you feel, and what you say you want. It is the essence of what you think, feel, and want in your inmost being. What is your soul's sincere desire? What are your heart's fondest beliefs? What are the truths, the dreams, the values that motivate your life?

You may cry out, "Order! Order!" But all the time your soul may be delighting in confusion. Anxiety and excitement may be what your soul is really crying out for. And you may believe that the world is in a dreadful state.

You may pray, "God, give me health," but sickness may satisfy some very real need of your soul. And you may believe that it is not possible for you to get well unless you follow a careful and prolonged treatment of one kind or another.

You may say, "Father, I must have a job," but the responsibility and demands of a job may really be the last thing you want. And you may believe that times are hard, that you are too old, that you lack required skills, or any number of things.

But granted that human beings are complex and that it may be hard in any instance to determine just what we are thinking and feeling and wanting to be true, is it this—faith and desire—that shapes our world? Is there even a possibility that Jesus was right and that this can be true?

The rock we build on

Let us look once more at what the scientists tell us the world is like. The world is an infinite flux. It is a never-ceasing sea of motion, with waves becoming particles and particles becoming waves—all forming out of the infinite no-thing and returning into the infinite no-thing.

The cloud-shapes we call things, finite and transient, are constantly forming and vanishing. They may last for a long time, like mountains and stars, or for a short time, like dew and rosebuds, before they change.

If the world is really such a flux, such a concourse and stream of atoms and energy, if this is what is there, what then gives it the particular shape it seems to have to me? The real world—the abiding spiritual reality—has the shape God gives it, and I am satisfied to go along with the scientists that this is a vast, dancing river of light and power. But it is obvious the world has no such shape for me. I see it as green lawns, white houses, cool water, smiling faces, cheerful words, and all the rest of "the ten thousand things."

Reflection makes it clear that my world looks like what it looks like because I am what I am, because I have the mind I have, the senses I have, the faculties I have.

And every creature's world is like what it is like because every creature is like what it is like. How different my human-shaped world must be from a housefly's or a morning glory's!

The infinite flux takes infinite forms, not exactly the same for me as for you, though we are close. Not much the same for me as for the mockingbird in the mimosa tree down the road, singing by the light of the moon. Hardly at all the same for the mockingbird or me as for the sea anemone that waves its flowerlike fronds in the watery half-light of the ocean floor. And what form does the world take for some creature, say, on Sirius?

The world is as God made it—and God made it good. But the world takes its momentary seeming from the consciousness of its observer, as some of the world's greatest thinkers from Gautama Buddha to Immanuel Kant have taught.

It would appear that Jesus may very well have known what He was talking about.

This does not mean that the world is anything we may imagine it to be. The world we live in is not an imaginary one. We do not change it by creating a mental image of some other world we would rather be in. Nowhere did Jesus say, "According to your imagination, be it done."

Faith is not imagining. It is not seeing something that is not real. On the contrary, it is seeing to the very essence of reality. It is thinking and feeling to a reality that is there, but that ordinarily we do not see—as when a mystic sees an angel, or a scientist a law of nature, or a poet beauty no one else has glimpsed.

Faith is not making believe. It is believing and making. The difference between believe and make-believe is the difference between seeing things by sunlight and moonlight. Imagination may turn on a light, but faith turns on the power. When we think of imagination, we think of wings. When we think of faith, we think of a rock. Wings can carry us to new adventures, but it is upon the rock of faith that we build a life. We may soar on imagination, but we stand on faith. We walk on faith.

Faith is standing firm—or walking on. We live by our faith. Sometimes by imagination we may try to escape from living. Faith enables us to meet life honestly and courageously.

Sometimes we confuse courage and faith. But courage is not faith. Courage is the power to go forward when we are without faith, when we are afraid. Faith is the power to go forward without fear.

If we did not have faith, how much courage we would have to have! At nightfall, for instance, or at the onset of winter. But we have faith, and so we are not afraid.

And I observe that the birds and wild things of the wood— with no knowledge of how the earth turns on its axis and circles round the sun—have an awareness no less than ours that the sun has set only to rise again and that winter will turn once more to spring.

When you change, the world changes

Faith is a kind of knowing. But faith is more than the kind of knowing we do with the intellect, as when we reason that two plus two is four, or that the sun is a ball of hydrogen and helium 93,000,000 miles away—though knowing this may be more an act of faith than we are aware.

Reason and faith are both ways of laying hold of truth. Reason is the way of the mind, faith the way of the heart.

Sometimes we think of faith and reason as if they were contradictory. But the greatest of Moslem teachers, al-Ghazali, said, "Reason is God's scale on earth." And Aristotle said, "Reason more than anything else *is* man."

What a disorderly world it would be if we could not count

on reason to reveal truth! Reason always reveals the truth. But reason works from premises to conclusions, so it cannot go beyond its premises. Give reason one and one, and it always comes up with two. Give faith one and one, and sometimes it touches infinity.

Reason is the great electronic computer God gave to Man. It gives a perfect answer, but it can figure out its answer only from the facts it has at hand.

Most of the time we have so few facts that reason has to present us with limited notions of truth, with part-truths. For a long time, reason concluded that the earth was flat. And all the best educated and most intelligent people believed this. In fact, it was still a dangerous heresy not to believe it long after Copernicus had demonstrated that it was not true. Today reason has concluded that the earth is round. And all the best educated and most intelligent people believe this. In fact, I can think of few heresies that would seem to most of us so bad as to doubt this.

Also, for a long time reason concluded that matter is a continuous substance. Today it has concluded that matter is made up of minute particles that are vast distances apart comparatively.

Also, for a long time reason concluded that combustion occurs because combustible materials contain a substance called phlogiston, which they give off when they burn. Today reason has concluded that combustion occurs when certain elements combine with oxygen. For many years, however, all the best educated and most intelligent people believed in phlogiston. Even the discoverer of oxygen, Joseph Priestley, believed in it. It was a reasonable belief.

Reason's truths, like the world of things that it tells about, are always changing. They change because they are always incomplete. They are always incomplete because reason is always working from incomplete data. It gives us truths in the light of the facts, but we never have all the facts. And when new facts come to light, reason demands new truths.

It is interesting to note that scientific truth depends on a fundamental contradiction. For scientific truth to be valid, our senses have to report the truth about the world around us. For it is from data gathered by our senses that scientists arrive at scientific truth. But if scientific truth is valid, the world our senses report to us is not the real world at all. For the world of particle-waves, which the scientists tell us is the real one, is certainly nothing like the common-sense world of blue skies and green fields our senses report to us.

Yet in spite of this basic contradiction, science works. Does it work the way all things work, because we think and feel and want it to be true?

The assumption that the earth was flat worked once, just as the assumption that it is round works now. The assumption that matter was continuous substance worked once, just as the assumption that it is made up of particles works now. The assumption that combustion was caused by phlogiston worked once, just as the assumption that combustion is caused by oxygen works now.

How can this be?

Is it not worth consideration, at least, that it is because life is consciousness, and our world always takes the shape of what we think and feel and want to be true?

What do you believe to be true? What do you want to be true?

If you want to change your life and your world, change what you think and feel and want to be true. When you change, your world changes.

When you change, the world changes!

What a thought this is!

Consider, for instance, walls

When you change, the world changes!

Think of it from the standpoint merely of gravity. Science teaches that every particle of matter exerts an influence on every other particle. You cannot move without moving the world. Raise your hand and you jog the sun. Turn this page and in the Great Nebula of Andromeda, almost a million light-years away, there must be answering motion.

Such changes are, of course, imperceptible.

But change your thinking, and you change the very shape of the world you live in. Change what you think and feel and want to be true, and truly you will find that the "old things are passed away; behold, all things are become new"—yes, all that you are and the world is.

Put your hand in the hand of faith, and walk on.

Faith and reason walk hand in hand, but where reason comes to a halt and can only turn on itself in questioning circles, faith walks on into an unknown land.

For faith is more than knowing with the mind. Faith is knowing with the heart.

So faith can go to the heart of what is there. Faith can go through the facts that constitute the surface of things and reach to the truth that is at the core of being.

Consider, for instance, walls.

The fact is that walls are walls—solid, impervious, hard, concrete. But the truth, even the scientific truth, is that walls are nothing mostly, mainly empty space. Walls are made up of particles—the scientists tell us—and these particles are almost as far apart relatively as are the planets. Walls are merely energy dancing on emptiness, more full of perpetual motion than the waves and winds of the sea.

And the fact that walls are particles is only part of the truth about walls. For the truth is that walls are thought. Walls are mind-stuff. In this aspect, the merest fancy—the chance vagary of the moment—has as much reality as a wall.

For what is a wall but a fact that my senses reveal to me concerning a portion of the world around me? The nerves in my eyes and in my hands, if I get close enough, report to me some sensations that I call a wall. Yet what are my senses but instruments of my mind? And the sensations they report— are they not the merest thought-stuff?

We know that many kinds of radiation penetrate a wall. Had I only organs sensitive to this invisible light, walls would be as transparent as glass. And had I only the power to synchronize the motions of the particles of my body with the motions of the particles of a wall, I could step through the wall as easily and harmlessly as I step through a summer shower.

Are all the walls that loom around us only in our mind? And is faith the power to see through the walls and step through the walls into a freer, wider, more beautiful world, a world closer to the eternal real?

Seeing the spiritual reality

Perhaps faith sees things in more dimensions than we customarily see things in. Faith is not making believe that things are not what they appear to be to our senses or to science; faith is believing yet more. It is seeing to a higher reality.

63

Faith is like looking at a mere point of light in the night sky and knowing that it is a world.

It is like watching a wave burst in foam along the sand and knowing that the sea is the boundless deep.

It is like looking at the fields and hills of earth and knowing that the earth is a star.

Faith is standing in the winter snow or the summer drought and seeing the fields green with wheat. Even more, it is making preparation for the harvest.

For faith involves action. There is no faith without works. Faith always works. Faith is works. The essence of faith is that we live by it. Faith shapes us and shapes our life.

Is faith a kind of seeing?

Yes, but more than seeing. Faith holds firm where we cannot see.

Faith does not look for signs. Faith may be strongest when signs are fewest.

Faith is a certainty, based not on outward conditions but on inward convictions.

Faith is knowing that the sun is shining when the sky is overcast with clouds.

Faith is knowing where the trail is when we are in the woods at night.

Faith is the kind of knowing a helmsman has as he pilots his ship through reefs in a raging storm.

"I hope you know where all the rocks are," cries the frightened passenger.

"I don't know that," says faith, "but I know where the deep water is."

Faith is Elijah digging ditches when there is not a cloud as large as a man's hand in the sky.

Faith is Marie Curie following the trail of radium even to the door of death.

Faith is Job affirming, "Though he slay me, yet will I trust in him."

Faith is Thomas Edison doggedly trying substance after substance till suddenly there is light.

Faith is Jesus praying, "Father, I thank thee that thou hast heard me. And I knew that thou hearest me always," before ever He uttered the cry, "Lazarus, come forth."

Faith is anyone who cries out to a world of suffering, "God is love."

Faith is the soul as it plummets through the unknown, affirming like a psalm of praise, "Underneath are the everlasting arms."

Faith cries, "If I may but touch his garment," and reaches out, knowing that His garment never trails outside the reach of prayer.

"Peace! Be still!" says faith when fear awakens it and rebukes the wind and waves. For faith knows that at the center of all the storms in the world is perfect peace; and when it makes itself one with peace, when it thinks and feels and wants peace, only peace can appear.

Faith looks at sickness, but reaches beyond to the pool of wholeness—the infinite, abiding, ever-renewing life of God.

Faith looks at lack, but reaches beyond to the power and the substance, the riches and glory welling forth from the eternal fountain.

Faith looks at inharmony, but reaches beyond to the everlasting order that beats at the heart of being, to the love that made and the law that governs all that is, to the truth on which all other truths rest for support.

Faith looks at things as they seem to be, but sees yet more. Faith is the world seen not with the senses but with the spirit. And spirit discerns spiritual reality.

Faith sees things even as God made them—in that day when (it is written) He made Man in His image and (it is written) He looked and "saw everything that he had made, and behold, it was very good."

The power to touch reality

Faith may be blind, based on surrender and dependence, like a child's faith in its mother or a soldier's faith in his captain when he goes on a mission because he has been ordered to go.

Blind faith believes that there is a power—call it God or Jesus Christ—that can heal and help us. We have to turn to this power and cry out, "Lord, I believe; help thou mine unbelief."

Faith may be understanding, like the faith a scientist has that a rocket will follow a certain path, or the faith one of us has in a friend. It is based on knowledge that certain principles are at work, that certain forces are present, that the universe is the good work of the good One.

This is the faith I pray to have:

I am one with God.

God is good.

I am one with good.

God's good is at work in my mind, in my body, and in my world even now, even though I do not see it, even though I do not feel it.

Good has to be in my world because God is there. And God is good.

Affirmative prayer is the prayer of understanding faith. The purpose of such prayer is not to help us imagine more desirable conditions than the ones we find ourselves in; it is to affirm a higher reality.

Faith is the power to touch reality. And what is reality? It is the world God made and saw was good.

Faith is the power to reach through what seems to what is. Faith is the power to stand firm with God, with the good.

Faith is knowing, when you are sick, that you are God's child, made in God's image—perfect, whole, alive, and strong.

Faith is knowing, when you are in need, that you are God's child, heir to God's kingdom, blessed with God's riches.

Faith is knowing, when you do not know where to turn, that you are God's child. Your life is in God's care. God is ever with you to guide and strengthen you.

Faith is knowing, when you are unhappy, that you are God's child, and God's joyous spirit is in you. God's love is yours to give and enjoy.

Faith is knowing, when your world seems confused, that you are God's child, one with God's peace, one with God's order. Divine wisdom is governing your life.

When we want and believe in life, we shall have life. When we want and believe in peace, we shall have peace. When we want and believe in joy, we shall have joy.

"According to your faith be it done to you."

This is the teaching of the Master.

your own world
THREE

With what measure will you measure?

How little that is truly meaningful, how little that gives meaning to you or your life, can be measured with a ruler or weighed in a balance or computed in foot-pounds.

You wake—and colors and sounds and tastes and smells sweep in on you like a sea. Winds of thought blow, blow through your mind. Trickles and streams and torrents of feeling pour over your heart.

How shall you measure these? How shall you weigh these?

The song you whistle as you shave; the tastes and smells of breakfast; the headlines in the paper; conversation over coffee; the feel of the air on your face and in your mind as you walk out the door; the exhilaration of early morning traffic—how many foot-pounds will these be?

The look on your wife's face when she looks at you—or loneliness? What ruler will you use to measure these?

What is the weight of a sunlit morning?

How many inches long is a rainy Sunday afternoon—or do you measure this in light-years?

How many foot-pounds will the idea exert that one day will harness the tides of the sea or move a planet into another orbit?

How shall I measure the breadth of mind? the power of an idea? the weight of authority? the length to which love may go? the height to which vision may rise? the depth of sorrow? the substance of a thought?

How shall I weigh truth? or joy? or fear? or anticipation?

Will you tell me in ounces how heavy or light your heart may be—or shall I listen for your tears or your laughter?

71

And the you-ness of you! Do you have a scale to measure that?

No, the realest things in life are not things that we measure or weigh or compute. For they are living things, and they can only be understood in terms of living.

Life is what you make it

The realest things in life are not the things that happen.

The things that happen are like places we encounter along the road—the bend, the ford, the pass, the town, the thicket, the valley, the forest, the fork, the shelter for the night.

All travelers come to these places, but how different is the journey each one makes.

Each person's world is personal. It cannot be measured in minutes or miles, but only in personal terms.

We happen to things more than things happen to us.

What we do at the river crossing—this is what matters much more than what the river crossing is like.

When we get to the forest, we shall find it full of trees—but is it also full of peace or full of fear? Is the forest the place where you lose yourself or find yourself?

The forest is what we make it to be.

The Hindus tell the story of a young man who came to a god to put his wisdom to the test. The young man brought a bird hidden in his hand and said to the god, "Is the bird in my hand alive or dead?" If the god said, "Alive," the young man intended to tighten his hand and kill the bird; if the god said, "Dead," the young man intended to open his hand

and show the bird alive.

The god said, "It is as you make it to be."

The world is as we make it to be.

Some people have interpreted this to mean that the world is a dream world, a world that exists only in our thought, an illusion, maya.

Not at all.

It is an enchanted world, a magic world, but not a dream world.

And the world is not like the bird the young man had in his hand, for we could not kill it if we wished.

The world is alive.

The world is as much alive as you and I are.

I bow to trees when I walk through a forest and the trees bow back.

We do not talk, but I think we have come to understand each other. For many years I used to lie under a certain willow tree and expect a dryad to step out and speak to me. Then I realized that my tree was probably waiting for a tree to grow out of me so that she could communicate with it. Since then we have understood each other better.

I have grown to see that most communication is not words—words often hide rather than disclose. The communication that goes on between trees and human beings, beasts and human beings, fields and human beings, mountains and human beings, seas and human beings, stars and human beings, God and human beings—this is not a matter of words, but "deep calleth unto deep" at levels where we seldom go. At these depths we that seemed separate mingle and flow as one.

Solitary wandering is such a deep.

Love is such a deep.

Prayer is such a deep.

Silence is such a deep.

These take us to the root of the tree of life. Out at the ends of the twigs the leaves twirl and grow, each separate, each free—but down at the root they are one.

We get to thinking that nothing is alive but us and things like us—carbon compounds burning in oxygen.

There is nothing that is not alive.

There is nothing that you cannot give yourself to and there is nothing that cannot give itself to you.

There is nothing that you cannot communicate with and that cannot communicate with you—and commune with you—and unify with you. There is nothing that you cannot make yourself part of, for there is nothing you are not part of. There is nothing that you cannot get into the heart of—if you get it into your heart.

Ask sailors how alive the sea is, and woodsmen how alive the woods are, and ploughmen if their fields are alive or not.

And O you astronomers—you of the light-years and spectroscopic bands—has no star ever opened its heart to you and have you never opened your heart to a star? Has the moon never wooed you till you laid your secret soul upon her bosom? Has the sun never opened its golden eyelid and gazed at you, mind into mind, till you were filled not with words and computations, but with a vision of light?

If not, you are no true lover of the truth, but only an astral mechanic, and the universe you hope to find with your telescope and computations will keep her true nature forever hidden away from you.

You will never uncover her nakedness. You will never know her, never.

This is an enchanted world

This is an enchanted world, not a dream world. There is a world of difference between the two!

It is not a world where we are constantly faced with illusions, but a world where we are perpetually surprised by truth.

The world is alive. Being alive, it changes and grows.

In a living world, would we expect to find a dead truth?

No, truth is alive too. Truth, too, changes and grows.

Do not expect to catch truth in a box and pin it on a board to display in a museum.

It is a caterpillar truth.

Tomorrow it will be a butterfly truth.

And if your butterfly truth falls out of the sky and its delicate wings turn to dust, do not despair. From the ashes of dead truths, truths yet more radiantly winged will rise and fly.

Would I catch the wind in a basket or the sea in a bowl or the light of the stars in a mirror?

How shall I catch the wind? I shall breathe it in and breathe it out again. That is how I catch the wind.

How shall I catch the sea? I shall feel its salty tides in the blood that beats through my veins. That is how I catch the sea.

How shall I catch the light of the stars? In the thoughts that glow in my mind. That is how I catch the stars.

There are many people who will tell you that the world is not enchanted. They will tell you you can weigh it in scales and measure it with rulers. But I tell you that what you have weighed has already changed, and the scales with it, before you set down your musty figures in your dusty books.

Did you weigh a cloud? The cloud has fallen as rain. And the rain has sprung up as a vine. And the vine has put forth flowers. And the flowers have grown into fruit. And you have plucked the fruit and eaten it. And you are yourself that cloud that you thought to weigh.

All life is the wedding feast of Cana, and when the Master of Life is invited in, though we draw but plain water from water jars of stone, we shall drink the wine of spirit and cry out to the bridegroom, "You have kept the best wine until now!"

Whatever you think it is, it is something more

Can you believe that the world is less than enchanted?

In a dream world we wander among illusions, but in an enchanted world we soar among truths.

If you think you know what the world is like, it is you who live in a dream world. Whatever you think it is, it is something more.

The next breeze that blows through your slumbers will bring new smells and sounds you have not heard before.

The world is no illusion.

To say that our world is an illusion is like saying that the world we see by moonlight is an illusion because it is not the world we see by sunlight.

If we dove to the bottom of the sea and looked at the sea from its watery depths, the sea we saw would be no more an illusion than if we looked at it from a sandy beach or the deck of a ship or an airplane high above its surface.

The way you look is not an illusion. It is as real as anything else about you. It changes from moment to moment as you change, as I change. But it is the way you look—from where I am.

I have to learn to tell truth from illusion. I live by truth; I perish by illusion. All living things must be able to tell what is true from what merely seems to be true; else they perish. The fox must learn to tell the secret snare; the desert wanderer the mirage.

The world is full of wonder, full of wonders. As strange and unexpected as dreams may be, reality is stranger yet and much more unpredictable.

Most of us accept the world as it appears to be, as the world would have us believe it is.

"The world is flat," all the bright people say. So for thousands of years we accept the world as flat. We cannot even conceive anything more to say about it.

"The world is round," all the bright people say. So for thousands of years we accept the world as round. We cannot even conceive anything more to say about it.

From being two-dimension people we have grown to three-dimension people. After a while we will grow to four-dimension people. Then we will say something more about the world—something we cannot even conceive to say about it now.

"A fact is a fact is a fact," some of us like to say.

But facts are just the limitations we settle for. Today's facts are yesterday's fancies and tomorrow's fallacies.

Some of us like to think of ourselves as realists. But that just means that we like to accept things as they seem to be.

Realists have common sense. But often they turn out to be wrong; someone comes along who has more sense than is common.

"Face reality," we like to say. But where do we face to face reality? North, east, south, or west? Up or down? In or out?

What is real?

The realest things in life are not the things that happen. Things happen. But what will turn out to be realest about them is how they happen to you.

Truth always happens

Truth always happens—in a sense fortuitously. We never make it happen.

We have no power to make it happen.

In a sense, we stumble onto it. We look—and there it is.

But we only stumble onto it because we have been looking for it; we have combed the mountain in our never-tiring search.

I am sure that people who never thought of looking for them have stumbled onto treasures—but whenever we read of treasure being stumbled onto, we usually find that the lucky stumbler has spent a lifetime in the treasure's search.

I have read of people coming effortlessly on great new insights in a dream. There the new light was, a gift from the gods. But always, when I read further, I learned that the one who had had the dream had given all his waking hours, sometimes for many years, to the pursuit of his dream.

How could an orderly universe have it otherwise? Would we like to believe that our future happiness depends on chance or fate or divine design and not on merit or effort?

From ability believed in and practice persevered in—from

this most great achievement springs.

The achievement, when it comes, may be effortless—but only because of the years of effort.

There is the fruit hanging on the tree—see how ripe and luscious, beautiful and perfect! But oh, the years of toil that brought it to that ripe perfection; the sending down of roots into the unyielding soil, the sending up of branches into the unstable air, the winters and summers, droughts and storms, winds and sun, the slow growth, twig on twig and leaf on leaf!

God does not play games of chance with us. All blessings are boons—but we must prepare to receive them. When the Guest knocks at the door—unless we have made the chamber ready—He cannot stay in our house.

And let us think no longer of the Guest as This or That—whatever we have named our God—for God is all and any good.

Not by our narrow notions

Are we saved by grace? Are we saved by merit?

Are we saved by faith? Are we saved by works?

Such arguments are meaningless. They beggar truth, the world, and God. For truth, the world, and God are not limited by our narrow notions about them. God is not concerned with our inconsistencies; God is great enough to include them all.

Are we mind? Are we body?

Are we spiritual beings living in a spiritual world? Are we physical beings living in a physical world?

Is the cause of events material? Is the cause of events in our thinking?

Do we have free will? Are our lives predetermined?

Is the world that our senses reveal real? Is the real world one that our senses do not reveal at all?

This is a world where contradictions abound.

Is the ultimate physical reality a particle? Is the ultimate physical reality a wave?

Oh, say the scientists, the ultimate physical reality is a wave that acts like a particle and also a particle that acts like a wave.

Here they have hit much closer to the truth than many religionists do.

We live in a world of opposites, but opposites are only ways of looking at what is.

We have two ways of looking at everything that is. Is this why we have two eyes—to remind us of this truth?

If we seek far enough into chance and probability, into the seeming haphazardness of nature, we come at last on scientific truth—on nature's laws. If we go far enough with nature's laws, we come back at last to entropy tables, to becoming, to running down, to mere statements of probability, to the principle of indeterminacy.

This is an interesting principle. To put it in big words, in the submicroscopic world of ultimate stuff, any observations we make in order to get the necessary data to determine future behavior disturb what we are observing in an unpredictable way, and therefore our data become useless in the very act of obtaining them.

This means several things.

First, when we look at the stuff the world is made of, we

change it just by looking—no surprising discovery to many of us, who have always believed that things tend to become what we see them to be!

Second, just because we know how things are behaving at this moment, we cannot be certain how they are going to behave a moment from now. Anything we say about reality is not true all the time.

So, here at the very core of things, we find them influenced by thought—by the act of the observer! And in the very citadel of determinism is the principle of indeterminacy!

Follow freedom far enough, and it brings you up against the law. Follow law, and it leads you to freedom.

I am free.

This I believe with all my heart.

If there is any meaning and if there is any dignity and if there is any importance to anything that is, then I am free. If I am not free, then all that seems to have meaning and dignity and importance becomes only the rattle of machinery—even if the machine be God's!

All the brave acts of heroes and all the selfless acts of saints—even the Cross—become merely the motions of puppets in a puppet show.

Though the whole world be the tent and God the Puppeteer, it is still only a puppet show—hardly worth the price of admission.

No, I am free!

Yet I believe in law. I believe I live in a world governed by law. I believe in a law of cause and effect. I have only to look at where I am standing to see that I came here by steps. I see that I am what I am today because I was what I was yesterday and the day before that and the day before that. And what I am today will determine what I will have become tomorrow.

The Easterner, overwhelmed by this notion, saw himself caught as on a wheel and brought forth his law of karma.

Karma means simply "deed."

You—the you you know as you and call by your name—are, says the East, nothing but the traces of your deeds.

As to the real You, the You God made, the You that began in the beginning, there is nothing that can be said about this. It is as God is; it is a portion of the Infinite, impossible to describe, almost impossible to imagine.

To understand what the East teaches about you and your karma, imagine a rope.

In the rope a knot is tied.

After a time the knot comes untied and yet another knot is tied.

Each knot is new—or is it the same one tied anew? It takes the form it has because the previous knot gave the rope an irresistible twist in that direction.

But the rope is always the same.

You are the rope.

And you are the knot that is tied again and again in the rope.

A clean slate

An Englishman, John Locke, said that you are like a clean slate. He used the Latin term and called you a *tabula rasa*. Interestingly, this notion of *tabula rasa*, or "clean slate," is the one the Founding Fathers of the American Revolution had. They got it from Locke. It is because he believed this—that all people are composed of the same mental or spiritual stuff—that Thomas Jefferson wrote, "All men are created equal." So this notion lies at the core of the way of life we Americans live, whether we know it or not.

The Buddhists say of you that you are, in your essence, a void.

But Genesis tells us that Spirit moved upon the face of the void. Life began to write on the clean slate.

You have thought thoughts—each thought has left its trace on the slate.

You have spoken words—each word has left its trace.

You have done deeds—each deed has left its trace.

You are these traces; you—the person—this is what you are. Except for this, there is only a clean slate.

You are the prisoner of what you have been. You are wrapped in the chains of causality.

The East sees you as caught in Karmic law. Islam sees you as under the spell of Kismet. Orthodox Christianity sees you as predestined to sin or to be saved. Scientific materialism sees you as a minor cog in a mechanistic universe, and lectures about determinism, behaviorism, conditioned reflexes.

What are you? You are what your genes and your infantile environment determined you would be, the modern psychologist tells me.

There is no question he is right. I am my genes. I am my infancy. I do not believe that any reasonable human being questions their molding influence.

But, likewise and paradoxically, I do not believe that any reasonable person seriously questions that he or she is free.

The answer we arrive at depends on the point from which we start.

Some truths come from the inside out, some from the outside in.

Determinism. This is an outside-in truth.

Free will. This is an inside-out truth.

All the great inconsistencies resolve themselves this way.

Take time and eternity. Can there be a beginning or an end? When we look outside, we see only beginnings and ends. Each beginning has an end, which is a beginning, which has an end, which is a beginning.

When we look inside, we see eternity—no ends, no beginnings, a state of being, not becoming; for we come not on circumferences but to the center, the Immortal Self. Inside, what person is there who does not feel immortal?

A city called Kansas City

I live in a city called Kansas City, Missouri. In my city there is a street called State Line. I have only to walk across this street, only to walk a few steps west, and I am in Kansas.

But suppose I do not know how to turn west. Suppose I can only face east. Then I may still get to Kansas, perhaps—but oh, what a weary journey, how many seas and continents and difficulties lie between me and my far-off goal!

Ask my east-facing neighbor how far it is to Kansas, and he may tell you, "I doubt that you can ever reach there at all."

Sometimes, when I read about the sidereal universe, with its whirling worlds on worlds of stars, with its astronomers who tell me about light-years and hundreds of light-years and hundreds of millions of light-years, I wonder if they are just not looking out of the wrong end of their telescopes, as it were. Just looking in the wrong direction. I don't mean east or west, of course, but a direction in which we have not yet learned how to look.

It has only been a few hundred years since our forefathers thought that if they sailed west a few hundred miles they would fall off the edge of the world.

We are looking out into space and sailing out into space. I wonder what it will be like to look "in" into space and to sail "in" into space. I do not know how, but some day some bright human being is going to be able to.

Whenever I see something as far away as a million light-years, I am sure we are just looking in the wrong direction. I want to say, "Turn around." But we have not yet learned how to turn around in a mental or spiritual sense as easily as we have in the physical.

One of these days, however, someone will come along who looks in the right direction, and there the universes will be, Sirius and the Great Nebula in Andromeda and the Hercules Star Cluster and all the rest of it, just a step across the street, so to speak.

I wonder if there are any opposites that do not resolve themselves into each other.

East is west, and straight lines turn out to be the longest as well as the shortest distance between two points.

In the world of thinking, if we carry any line of reasoning far enough we end up ad absurdum, as Zeno did in his famous proof that a moving arrow does not move.

To say that an arrow moves, said Zeno, we have to say that it moves in the place where it is or the place where it is not. But to say that it moves in the place where it is is a contradiction, for that is the same as saying it is at rest. And to say that it moves in the place where it is not is impossible, since nothing under any circumstances can be where it is not.

On the other hand, if we go far enough into the absurd, will we not come out like Alice in Wonderland, into an extremely reasonable view of things?

Hot and cold are, in the extreme, indistinguishable to sense, I understand. Whether the world ends by flood or fire seems immaterial, I think most of us will agree.

Seek hard enough for pleasure and you will come to boredom, which is pain. Press deeply enough into pain and you will come to oblivion, which is peace.

Sharpen a knife enough and you have no edge at all.

Even hate and love are not as separate as they at first may seem. When we hate anything enough, we become one with it as surely as we become one with it when we love it enough. Sometimes when we hate greatly, our hate is a mask under which we hide the love we are afraid to own.

What then is right?

What are we to believe?

We live in a world where we cannot be concerned about contradictions, inconsistencies, and paradoxes. For in this world truth is one and many at the same time.

The world is the Infinite creating infinity out of itself—and it cannot be bound.

The One is, but many are its forms.

Look for it with all your heart and with all your mind and with all your strength—and you may find it has given itself to you.

For truth is the hound of heaven who pursues you till you take him captive.

Insist on too much freedom and you will find yourself in bonds. And when you have put yourself in bond to all, you may find you have the only freedom there is.

Refuse to accept, decline to be bound

Occasionally men and women appear who refuse to accept what we accept just because it is the accepted fact. They decline to be bound by what the rest of us meekly submit to. They do not find the truth comfortable merely because the rest of us have conformed to its shape.

Some of our most revered truths they toss into the ash can. Some of our most imposing impossibles they turn into fact.

In the physical sciences, how they have sent the old truths tumbling. In the arts, they have shown us we do not even see what we look at. About ourselves, they have disclosed new worlds. As to religions, think what they have done in the last hundred years to almost universally accepted beliefs.

Most of us, of course, go on in the old way. We accept the same limitations our fathers did.

Evolution is always hard.

Growth takes doing.

A great French cynic has said, "Man's first instinct is to sit down."

But we cannot sit down for long. Evolution is a law of life. Life is growth. Nothing alive stands still. Of all the facts we see in the world, none is so obvious and universal as change.

Whether we move slowly, resisting, or rapidly, seeking, we are going to surpass ourselves. We are evolving. Some of us move far ahead of the crowd.

Jesus, for instance, is so far ahead of us in His powers and in His notions of what is true that He seems almost like a member of another race. "God!" we say of Him. And we are right.

But did He not say, "Is it not written in your law, I said, Ye are gods?" Did He not say, "The works that I do shall he do also; and greater works than these shall he do"? Did He not say, "Ask, and it will be given you"? Did He not say, "According to your faith, be it done to you"?

What manner of teachings are these that upset every comfortable notion we have about ourselves! What manner of teaching is this that tells me I am going to heal the sick, multiply substance, love my neighbor as myself, raise the dead, and even raise my own body from death—in short, have the powers of a god!

Yet the fact is that discarders and innovators like Jesus are not solitary mutations. We are all going to come to where they are—yes, every one of us—and we are going beyond them.

There are no limits to what we may grow to be. We are made in the image of the Infinite.

Unless you are happy with your pains and your pettiness, it is time to arise and be about the business you were made for—surpassing yourself.

If ever there was a time right for such work, it is this time you were born in. If ever a time said, "Accept no limits, change, grow, come up higher," it is this time.

No easy formulas, no certain ways

There are no easy formulas that add up to new faith, no certain ways to find it. Yet there are steps we can take.

Jesus could heal because it was easy for people to believe in Him. They could see Him. They could hear Him speak. They could feel the healing love in His touch.

Jesus Christ can heal still—"if thou canst believe."

We have to believe.

And it is not enough to say we believe; to accept with our feeling, but deny with our reason; to believe with one small portion of our mind and heart and disbelieve with the rest. The faith that makes us whole is the sum of what we think and feel to be true.

Faith must involve the emotions. It is not enough to think, "Health!" and go on feeling sick. Faith must involve reason. It is not enough to affirm, "Health!" and go on thinking, "I can't get well!"

Those who were healed in Jesus' time believed with all their heart and all their mind and all their strength that they could be healed.

In our time many of us do not have this kind of faith. We have been educated out of it. Our reason holds us back from following our hope.

What we really have faith in, we believe with our mind as well as with our heart, with our reason and our feeling.

We believe, for instance, that the sun will rise tomorrow. There is no part of us that holds back from believing this. Our reason does not say, "I am not sure," nor does our heart say, "I wonder."

We always have the deepest faith in things we think and feel to be so true that we are not even conscious we have faith in them.

For instance, I believe that my home is still where I left it when I came to work this morning. I believe that the stairs will lead to the front hall if I go down them, and if I walk out of the door, I will not be in Tanzania or on the moon. I believe that you will not suddenly change into another creature. Such beliefs I accept without even thinking about them. But they are beliefs!

Suppose we believed as strongly in health. Or plenty. That is the way we do believe in health when we have it. We just accept the fact of health; we just think and feel healthy. That is the way we believe in plenty when we have that. The rich person does not affirm riches or pray for riches. He just thinks and feels rich.

Not what we say, but how we live shows what we really have faith in. We may fool ourselves as to what we think and feel to be true. We may fool others. But we cannot fool life. For what we think and feel to be true becomes our life.

To change our world, we have to change what we think and feel to be true of our world. To reshape the world nearer to the heart's hoping, we have to grasp it with the mind and see that we have the power to shape it and that it has the power of being shaped.

Do you have doubts? Search for reasons to believe. "You will seek me and find me; when you seek me with all your heart I will be found by you." If you do not give up, you yet will answer, "Yea!" to life. The universe conspires to bring you to fruition. Everyone has doubts, but also does not everyone have times when he has intimations that he is more than anything he has settled for?

Is there anyone who has not, at least for moments, found powers he did not know he had?

Is there anyone who has not seen things happen for which he could find no reasonable explanation?

Sometimes these are very small things. A man says a prayer and is led to find something he had not before been able to find. He speaks a word of order, and a machine begins to work that would not work. He gets quiet, and an idea that had been eluding him suddenly appears.

Everyone has had such experiences.

Sometimes they are large, as when a healing occurs where to all visible expectation there was no hope of one.

When such things occur, some of us may shrug and say, "Coincidence!" Others of us may say, "Miracle!" and give thanks.

But we have all witnessed or experienced such things, and they are a starting point for faith.

More than we settle for

Life is more than we settle for. There is a higher reality. There is a power beyond what we ordinarily believe to be our own, beyond what we ordinarily believe to be operating. This power is accessible. At times we all touch it—or let it touch us.

The power that faith connects us with is not really an extraordinary power, for it works continually in expected ways; only we accept these daily manifestations matter of factly, as if ordinary things were not just as strange and wonderful as extraordinary things are. Everything there is— atoms, comets, snow, alligators, grass, rocket ships, birth, growth, life, the functioning of our body, the movement of the stars—is the result of this power. This power is flying as thought through our mind. It is stirring as love through our heart.

But occasionally it does show itself, not in these daily happenings we have lost the power to feel amazement at, but in some unlooked-for way.

The Christmas rose blooms in the winter's ebb!

Then we fall on our knees in the stable, for a moment aware that life is not dull and ordinary, a thing of laws and tables, easily explained and perfectly predictable; but life is a wonder and a mystery, the spilling-over, ever-flowing joying of an unspeakable power!

The world is the work of God, and everything in it is the work of God.

God is good.

God is love.

God is intelligence.

When we think and feel this to be true, our world has to become the kind of world that is the only kind of world love and intelligence can create.

The world has the shape of intelligence, oh round and reasonable globe! The world has the shape of love, oh infinitely varied loveliness!

What made the man Jesus different from the rest of us is that He never doubted for a moment that the world is made by love and intelligence—no, not when He saw men mistreating one another, not even when they scourged and crucified Him.

He saw that the world is something more than it seems to be to our less than loving gaze. He saw that the hatred and the cruelty and the pain are not the truth about it. He saw to a meaning that eludes us, a vision of a truth more glorious than any our eyes can see—except perhaps for moments or in glimpses.

But these moments and these glimpses are faith. To have faith is to see beyond all false appearances to the truth of goodness.

The good is there, whether we have the faith to think and feel through to it or not. The world is the work of a goodness beyond even our power to imagine what such goodness is.

O God, sometimes I sense how great You are! But I have no words. I do not even have thoughts.

Did I call You love? It is not enough.

Did I call You intelligence? It falls an infinity short.

Yet I listen, and from time to time I think I catch a word. I yearn, and there are times when I think I have almost touched the hem of the robe of reality.

The world is the imagining of a mind beyond my mind's imagining. The world is the upwelling of a heart past even my heart's power to dream.

Yet in the image of this mind beyond mind and of this heart beyond heart, I, too, am made! In me I have a power to be—yet more than I have ever dreamed or hoped or believed I might become.

Jesus said, "You will know the truth, and the truth will make you free."

What truth?

Any truth!

The truth about the universe. The truth about yourself. The truth about God.

We learn the truth about gravitation. And oh, amazing world! Gravitation is what binds men to the earth. But when they learn the truth about it, they fly!

I learn the truth about my emotions. I see that I am driven by hates and fears I did not even know I had. But when I come to understand them, I use the very energy they generate to build my world of love.

I am a child of God.

This is the truth about me.

When I come to think and feel this truth; when I come to believe it clear through, with my mind and my heart, my reason and my hope; when I know it not as a glimpse of something longed for but as the very substance and reality of what I am—then my world will have taken on the shape love and intelligence gave it when love and intelligence made it and "saw that it was good."

I am the child of God.

I am the child of love.

I am the child of intelligence.

I am the child of life.

"Beloved, we are God's children now; it does not yet appear what we shall be, but we know that . . . we shall be like him."

life's infinite variety
FOUR

One morning in my garden I asked God to bless every living thing. And God asked, "But what is not a living thing?"

First I thought of air—invisible, inert. But the air leapt into my mouth and became my living breath. The air became the red of my blood and in the secret furnace of my cells the air became the fire of life itself.

Then I thought of water—colorless, inert. But drinking the water, I thought, "What is this body that drank the water? Is it not itself mainly water? This water that I drank is now the essence of my blood and tissues. When, then, is water merely water and when is it water of life?"

Then I thought of earth—brown, inert. "Earth," I thought, "is not living," and I kicked at the clods under my feet. And lo, the clods under my feet turned green and put forth leaf and stem and flower and the grain ripened in the ear. I took the ear, ground it, made bread out of it, and ate the bread. And the bread became the very stuff of myself, so that I could not separate that which was me and that which was earth. This which now was me had but a short time before been the clods of earth that I had kicked with my feet.

"Surely," I thought, "there is something that is not living." I thought of stones. But even with the thought I sensed the stirring in the stone, and I knew that the immovable, changeless stones were changing and moving, flowing no less than rivers, to become the living pith and bone of creatures yet unborn.

Oh, then I caught a vision of the world—not as dead and inert, but as living and alive!

Suddenly I saw that even the infinitesimal particles of which all things are formed—too small even to imagine, too small almost to conceive—are alive. I watched and I saw that they were dancing; I listened and I heard them singing.

I saw all the world of which I am part, and I saw that it is life, nothing but life. Everything is alive and has the power of life. Things pass from one phase to another, from one form to another, but they are always alive. There is no line between living and not living. Both are aspects of life, as breathing in and breathing out are aspects of breath. There is only the breathing in and the breathing out again.

We move through a world of opposites, but the opposites are not the reality, they are only aspects of reality. They are only reality as seen from this viewpoint—or that. The reality is One, and it is Life.

I thought of some of the opposites—of night and day, of evil and good, of hate and love. I asked Night, "What is Day?" And the Night answered, "I am Day, only seen from the other side."

I thought of living and not living, and I saw that life is not the opposite of death, as it is generally thought to be. Birth is the opposite of death. Is death then but the same door as birth, only seen from the other side?

Now we can see things only from where we stand. Can it be that we see only one side of all that is, as we see the moon?

Ah, if we could see life not from the viewpoint of the moment, but in the radiance of eternity!

We would see not night and day, but eternity; not yea and nay, but truth; not birth and death, but life; not good and evil, but God.

We are the namers. We give names to all things and try to describe them.

But when is a rose a rose?

When it is a seed? when it is a new plant green with spring? when it is a heart-shaped bud? when it is a full-blown bloom? when it stands thorn sharp against the winter snow?

The universe is the rose of God.

The universe is not the fixed and finished work of a Master Maker, who made it and the things in it as a watchmaker makes a watch. The universe is a living organism, unfolding from within, creatively expressing the creative Spirit of God, from the smallest particle to the largest galaxy continually breathing, growing, expanding through space and time and mind and spirit, with no end or limit to the possibility of development.

And I, too, am the rose of God.

When was I, am I, shall I be?

Of this that is my body now, how much was my body a year ago? Of the stuff that was my body twenty years ago, does a single atom remain the same?

As to my mind, nebulous, delicate, subtle, dancing with thoughts, how shall I make my thoughts stand still long enough for me to say, "*This* is my mind"? This very thought has altered the configuration.

Now from the viewpoint of the moment, I see my existence as an isolated fragment, beginning, ending; but, could I but look from the fixed center of being and take in the whole reach of reality, I would see that what seems to be a broken arc is really the perfect circle of eternity.

Is this what the Lord of living saw when He hung upon the mount? From that anguished, ultimate peak of experience, did He see things not one-sidedly but whole? Did He look past endings and beginnings, past every appearance of separateness, clear to the Animating Principle, and did He see that the Animating Principle was Himself?

And we, when we see things whole, shall we, too, not share the wholeness?

O living air, earth, water, breath, blood, flesh, O metamorphosing rocks, there is no beginning and ending, there is no living and not living. There is only the ever-renewing, ever-unfolding expression of infinite life.

Walking in my garden, I asked God to bless every living thing.

Even as I asked, I knew that in all the world there was not one atom that did not leap up in acknowledgment.

Life is a mystery

Life is a mystery.

God is a mystery.

We swim in life like swimmers in a sea, and all our senses quiver to its incessant surges, its tides and currents, its storms and calms.

We stir to life. We hear its trumpets and we rise and go. We hear a music as from beyond the mountains; it calls us, "Follow!" and we follow—by unknown ways we could not tell you of or ever find again.

Life is a mystery.

God is a mystery.

What else would we have them be?

How much less they would be if they were something we could comprehend!

God made life so that He Himself can live and delight in living. O mystery indeed where the Infinite can make itself yet infinitely more!

We try to comprehend the mystery—and this we must.

For sometimes through our night the beautiful bird of truth flies overhead, and once we have glimpsed it, even for a moment, we can never cease from searching for it and trying to make it our own. And we capture some marvelous creatures—comforts beyond our expectations, powers we never knew were there, knowledge and plenty and life and health.

We get out our rulers and computers, our radar and rockets, our scopes and hopes, all the curious snares and ingenious stratagems our clever minds have devised. But this quarry truth has wings and flies from beyond the mountains. Reason, keen hunter though he is, must run along the ground.

What is the world we live in?

A paradox—a mystery.

It is only by our senses and our reason that we know what it is like. Yet by our senses and our reason we have come to know that it is not at all like what our senses and our reason tell us it is like!

What is the sun?

A shining disk, as big perhaps as a saucer, that slowly moves across the sky from east to west each day?

A star, a flaming ball of hydrogen half a million miles across and 93,000,000 miles away, around which the earth revolves?

A spiritual prince, clad in light, radiating glory, guiding a fiery car in splendor through the heavens?

And the earth—is the earth an angel, cloud-winged and azure-haired, robed in a dewy mantle, crowned with a glowing crown?

We ride down the road of the unknown; time, forever new, strange, unforethought of, unrolls under the feet of our mount.

But this is no gentle gray that rocks us down the road—we make our journey astride a magic steed.

Not a horse but a pig! that galumphs us out into a muddy wallow.

Not a pig but a tiger! leaping fanged and clawed on a drowsy antelope.

A tiger, no! but the antelope! and we crouch beneath the tiger's spring.

Not an antelope, thank God, but an eagle! and we soar, ah, we soar!

What is at the inner core of things?

A mystery.

And what is at the outer edge of things?

A mystery.

And between the inner core and the outer edge, what is there?

A mystery.

The larger we make our circle of light, the more darkness it reveals.

Our minds are pioneers, newcomers set down in an unexplored country. We have to stake out a homestead in a wilderness, but the larger we make our clearing, the more there is to be cleared. Have we doubled what we know? We have also doubled what we do not know.

The work of a master artist

Life is the work of a Master Artist, with a Wisdom Heart and a Mind of Love. Creative Intelligence—God—did not make life as a poet makes a poem or an artist paints a picture. For a poem or a painting is finished and complete. But life is never finished and complete.

Life is alive.

Life lives and grows.

Do you see it as clouds? Or is it green and growing things? Or is it pink-white flowers? Or is it red, red fruit? Or is it bare black boughs? Or is it sunlight shining through the clouds?

However you see it and whatever you call it, it is not that but something more.

This is the essence of life—it is always something more.

There is no limit to what life is nor any end to what life may become.

It never began.

It will never end.

It springs out of the Infinite. But it is just as right to say that the Infinite springs out of it.

It is the ever-renewing, ever-unfolding expression of the Infinite. The Infinite becoming infinitely more.

The Infinite becoming infinitely more!

O rainbow river, changelessly changing, varying endlessly, forming forever, never the same, shapes without number, thoughts without ceasing, out of eternity into eternity, everlastingly rising and flowing, always new, original, strange!

Count all the stars in all the worlds.

Count all the flowers in all the summer fields.

Count all the rains of spring.

Count all the snows of winter.

Count all the waves that break in all the seas.

Count all the days and nights of eternity—you have not even begun to consider life's infinite variety. Life cries, "Yet more! Yet more!"

God thought, and God's thoughts were light. And the light shone through the infinite darkness, and darkness became the world of space and time.

God spoke, and God's words were law. And reason became the rule by which all that was and all that was not were to be measured, and order put its imprint on all that had been meaningless, and the chaos became the cosmos.

God lifted His hand, and the motion of His hand was power. And the power rolled forth in waves like a sea, like waves to break forever across a boundless deep. Eternity began to breathe, to pulsate in time's ceaseless rhythms, and the atoms began their deathless dance.

God felt in His heart, and the feeling in His heart was love. And love was less than the least and humbler than the humblest, so love could reach even through emptiness and into the heart of heartlessness. Love got down underneath everything that was obdurate and cold and warmed it from within, so that everything obdurate and cold broke open, not from outer blows but because it wanted to be open.

God laughed, and His laughter was joy. And His joy became the infinite variety of shapes that are His world—earth and stars, flowers and creatures, men and women and children, all the myriad things we know of and all the myriad things we do not know of. And the laughter of God goes on and on—for God is the everlasting joy of being rejoicing in its own becoming more, delighting in its own spontaneity—

and wherever the laughter of God sounds, there the forms of life appear and reappear and give birth to yet more forms.

The sea calls to the sailor

I love this world. It is my blood and brain and bone. I eat and drink and breathe it and it shapes even my dreams.

O lovely world I love, dear, dear I hold you! I grasp you to me as you grasp me to you—roughly, tenderly. I feel you close against my skin—wind, rain, hot and cold weather, rub of textures smooth and coarse—closer than skin, blood beating in my veins and the electric leaping in my brain! World, we are part and part of one another—the fire that is the stuff of stars and suns blazes up on my hearth and in my heart. So solid to my seeming, solid world, I build my life on you as if on a rock. But world, you are mere bright, tumbling waves and flow away under the touch of my mind, quicksilver, running water, empty air! the changeling child of fire and nothingness, all singing atoms and all dancing light— and I, too, singing atoms, dancing light—perpetual motion and unchanging change!

World, what are you then? Only another dream? How real a world to be no more than a dream? If you are a dream, to dream is to be real, and to be real is to dream—and is this not so?

The world is very real and very dear. Around us press its sights, sounds, shapes, smells, people, streets, traffic, towers, the heavens, all the lights of day and night, hills, rivers, fields, woods, lakes, and all the creatures that inhabit these. We are so occupied with waking, sleeping, dreaming, working, hungering, feasting, loving, hating, hunting, fleeing, fighting, thinking, birthing, and dying that we have no time for anything more. We have no wish for anything more. Sometimes we feel that we could go on with this forever.

Yet real as this world is and dear as this world is, I wonder if there has ever been anyone who did not have a sense of something somehow before he was born and of something somehow after he will have died?

I sense a press, a thronging of worlds. The Infinite One could not create less than an infinity of worlds. We live on the edge of worlds we do not see. Worlds so different I cannot even imagine them, yet worlds I somehow am not unfamiliar with.

I cannot put these worlds into words, not even for myself. I cannot conjure them up in terms of senses and dimensions. But how much even of this world cannot be put into words or measured in terms of senses and dimensions!

Much of the time I feel that this world is my native country. Yet at times I have a sense of another land and time—of a far country and wide seas between. Then I am as if I were an alien in an alien land. I stand like one who wakens from a dream, unable to remember what he dreamed but remembering that he dreamed.

The sea calls to the sailor. He hears it though far away. The tides are in his blood, and they rise and fall with the moon.

The sailor may plough and sow in fields that are far from the sea. By night he may shutter his window and sleep in a warm, soft bed.

But the sea will come calling, calling across the fields and the hills. From beyond the dunes of forever, the sea will come calling to him.

Then he will turn from his work. He will start up from his sleep. For he was made for seafaring, and he must be up and away.

We are all seafarers. Do you never stand on the shore?

You have come up to here

I know past any doubting that this world where now I find myself is not the country of my origin. Dearly as I love it, I am but an immigrant—perhaps that is why I love it so much. I journeyed here, though by a way I have no memory of.

Is there anyone who has never driven down a road and suddenly the country he was driving through was not the country lying round about him, but a strange and different country—yet for all its suddenness and unexpectedness, not an unexpected country! It is almost as if you somehow came up over the hills that hem round the mind and there, spreading out before you, was the native valley of the soul—warm, dear, shining, bringing always a sense of homecoming, always an intimation of perfection, always a feeling that you are about to go back where you belong, a sense of being for a moment in a world far more real and more familiar than the world of everyday.

It is always only for a moment—and in a moment you are driving back in the world of everyday.

A trick of the mind, you say, and dismiss it.

But is every day less a trick of the mind, less a state of awareness?

Or are there doors and windows in the mind that once in a while—who knows how or why?—blow open and then we find ourselves staring into worlds we knew were there but had for a time forgotten?

We have lived before and will live again.

Where? In this world?

Perhaps.

Certainly in a world not too unlike it.

When two Hopi Indians meet, they greet each other with the words, "So you have come up to here!"

This is the world you have come up to.

It is a world that has had experiences in it that are hard and experiences that have been easy. A world of challenges, opportunities, pleasures, pains, steps to take, and limitations to surmount.

It is a world where you have succeeded in part and failed in part, like everyone.

I cannot believe that the next world will be essentially different—oh, appearancewise, perhaps, but not essentially.

It will be the world you have come up to.

It will have you in it—yes, just as in this world, at its very center.

So it has to be the kind of world that someone like you can exist in and can grasp at your level of awareness.

Life did not begin with birth; we have come through aeons of experience beyond imagining. And here we are. In this! In this delightful, sometimes frightful, aching, delicious world!

You are on your way. Your way may carry you to strange and curious scenes, perhaps. Sooner or later, no doubt it will.

But whether it be a world of green skies and purple seas, of fields that lie on edge and hollow hills, or have no skies or seas or fields or hills at all, if thoughts find form and form becomes like thoughts there—still it will be a world where you will be at home.

It will be your world, a world where you can exist, a world

that you can grasp and lay hold of in your mind, and with your heart; a world—I have faith—where you can, as you have here, grow to be more than you have been.

When one is infinitely dear

But what am I in this vast scheme of things? In this immensity, what meaning can I have, who am so little?

Someone has said that if we came from another galaxy and flew through the Milky Way trying to find the Earth, it would be like flying down the Mississippi Valley looking for a grain of dust!

This speck, Me, peering out from under a small leaf, lost among other leaves on the floor of the great rain forest extending endlessly in all directions—what difference can I make? Even if there were a God, how could God find time for me, with all the stars and planets to look after?

But importance has little to do with size; meaning has little to do with dimension.

We feel so dwarfed by the dimensions of the starry world we live in, this is hard for us to grasp.

Importance and meaning are not physical measures, like pecks and pounds, but measures in the mind.

And how does the mind measure? What is large and small? What is near and far? What is of much value and of little?

Nothing makes any difference in terms of the physical universe. For here there is nothing—only the blind action of blind forces—nothing more—whirling centers of energy forming and dissolving. Indeed, not even this, for even this is a conceiving of my mind. Certainly there are no green fields, blue skies, stars and Milky Ways, dandelions, men and women.

Nothing makes a difference until I—and you—come into it. Only when we look at it and say "Green grass!" or throw ourselves down in it to loaf or write a poem or think about what it is—only then is anything important, because only then is any thing.

Things may not be thoughts, as some have thought; but without thought there is nothing—meaningless motion in meaninglessness—not even space and time—not until I—or you—say, "Look out there!" not until you—or I—say, "Wait a moment!"

Meaning, importance—these are in the mind. Nearness has nothing to do with space, but is of the heart. You may be nearer to some who are thousands of miles away than you are to others who live in the same house with you.

Do you love one son less because you have other sons? No matter how many sons you may have, you cannot love them all together more than you love any one of them, when you love that one with all your heart.

And you can love one of them with all your heart, yet love all the rest as much.

Love is not a loaf that must be broken into smaller pieces because there are more hungry mouths to feed. Love is the loaf that the Infinite breaks.

Is there one hungry heart to feed? There is enough and an infinitude left over.

Are there five thousand? And five thousand times five thousand? You shall not have baskets enough to gather up what remains.

God does not love ten thousand human beings more than He loves one. Ten thousand are no more than one when one is infinitely dear.

His sparrow . . . His star

Have you ever stood on the shore of a lake when the sun was shining across the water? If you have, you have seen that it sent its beam of light across the water straight to you.

Yet if someone else happened to be standing farther down the shore and you called and asked him if he saw the sun, he would say, "Yes, it is sending its beam of light straight to me." And no matter how many others happened to be scattered up and down the shore, each one would say, "It is sending its beam of light straight to me."

How much more God is than His creature, the sun!

God is the God of all the world. Go to the farthest end of space, and God is there. Go to the longest stretch of time, and God is there. Go to the highest reach of thought, and God is there. You cannot imagine a place where God is not.

Yet God is no less in you. There is no more of God in all the world than there is in you. God has as much time for you as for all His world. God has as much love for you as for all His world.

God is not something that is more or less.

God is.

God is here as much as there.

God is in this as much as in that.

Of the Infinite, how do you say there is less here or more there?

Things can be divided and may have to be divided.

But not Mind. Not Spirit.

Are the laws that govern light less there where a candle is shining than where Arcturus or Antares is shining?

Are the laws that govern falling objects less there when a feather falls than when a star falls?

The Intelligence that governs the stars in their courses is there to guide your course.

The Love that holds the Milky Way in its hand is there to take your hand.

The same Intelligence.

The same Love.

No less. No less concerned.

Nothing is more important than something else. The whole is not more important than its parts. The whole is important. Each part is important. For everything is infinitely important.

And this I believe—if the universe disappeared and there were nothing left but you—if you disappeared and there were nothing left but one atom—from that atom the universe would recreate itself again—and universes beyond our dreaming!

For every atom is an infinite potential. An atom is the Infinite focused at a single point.

An atom is as meaningful as a planet, a pebble as a mountain. There is that to which the pebble is a mountain and that to which the mountain is a pebble.

How strange a world it would be if whales meant more than goldfish, or elephants than butterflies, or lumps of coal than diamonds, just because they are larger–or if starlings meant more than eagles or hummingbirds, just because there are more of them.

Your girth is not the measure of your worth.

God is God of the infinitesimally small as much as God is God of the infinitely large.

When God thought up stars, that must have been a satisfying moment—how much love and joy in being must have flowed out from Him then!

But when God thought up daisies, that must have been a satisfying moment too. Or earthworms, what a triumph of creative ingenuity!

When God thought up the precession of the equinoxes, He must have felt that that was very good. But when He thought up leaves and babies, that was very good too!

I am sure God put a lot of Himself into His work when He thought up the sun and the moon.

But how much of Himself He put into His work when He thought up you!

God is in the midst of you.

God is in the midst of the starry heavens too.

One does not have more of God than the other.

Does God know when a star falls, making for a thousand years a conflagration in the sky?

God also knows when a sparrow falls.

You are the sparrow of God, and you are also the star of God.

The I of me

What is the I of me?

Sentient, thinking, conscious, I have meaning. Yes, I!

It makes a difference what happens to me.

I am only a part of the whole, but I am that for which the whole was made.

If God is my reason for being, I am God's reason for being. God cares for me.

There is probably nothing in all the world that cannot be looked at from opposing viewpoints. Certainly there are two ways of looking at me.

I am mind. I am body.

I am a physical being living in a physical world. I am a spiritual being living in a spiritual world.

I have free will. The events of my life are predetermined.

Even more amazing, both views are probably true—depending on your viewpoint.

Does the sun revolve around the earth? Does the earth revolve around the sun? It is equally right to say either—depending on your viewpoint.

Life has infinite aspects. How can you lay hold of it in finite terms?

It is like trying to tell me what the heavens are like by holding up a lighted candle.

What we are looking at is more than we can grasp at a glance.

Suppose I had to tell you what the sky is like without being able to turn my head. It would make a great deal of difference in what direction I was headed. For my view from the east would not be the same as it would be from the west—no less true, but a different view.

It might help all of us if occasionally something happened to turn our heads a little—if those who see things only from a material viewpoint had to look at things from a spiritual viewpoint, and if those who see things only from a spiritual viewpoint had to look at things from a material viewpoint.

The world can be explained in terms of spirit, in terms of

matter, in terms of mind, in terms of all of them, and in terms of none of them.

Which way are you heading? That will determine what you see.

What am I most like?

Am I most like a diamond, come perfect from the hand of my Creator, a glittering and flawless gem—is this what I am?

Though time may wear me like a jewel on its forehead, or fling me into a refuse heap where I lie lost and hidden, or draw me through a fire, or fasten me in the crown of a king, this I of me—does it remain unaltered, immaculate, shining in pristine splendor, as I was in the beginning, am now, and always will be, the same perfect diamond?

Or am I most like a river?

When you think of a river, what do you think of? The water, the banks, the course, the source, or the mouth? Someone has said, "You cannot step twice into the same river." A river flows. Perhaps this is as much as you can say. You may map its course, but this will change before you finish the map. A river is more force than a fixed thing. Step into it and you may be swept away.

A river is change. It changes, no matter how you look at it. Walk along the river, and it changes with every step; stand still, and it changes with every moment.

What am I then?

Conceive, if you can, something that is like a diamond— shining, flawless, always the same—and just as much like a river—changing, flowing, never the same—and you have caught a sense of the I of me.

Perhaps I am most like a song.

What is a song?

A song is a thought in the imagination of its composer, an unheard music of the mind.

A song is words and notes set down on a sheet of music paper.

A song is a sweet undulation of sounds for a little time in a certain place.

And a song is also the singer singing, a mind and body expressing themselves.

I am the song and the sound and the singer.

You will hear me again and again, in different keys, in different voices, whistled and chanted and hummed, sometimes only a few bars, sometimes sung over and over. The singer may sing imperfectly, yet I am always the same perfect song, imagined music in the mind of my Composer, written down in the Eternal's music book, flawless and complete.

I am God's song.

Listen for me.

You are God's song.

Listen.

God's free gifts

FIVE

A divine economy

I breathe into the air. Outside my window is a tree. The tree takes my breath, mixes it with water and sunlight, and makes green leaves. As it does this, the tree in its turn breathes into the air. I breathed out carbon dioxide, which the tree needs, but the tree breathes out oxygen, which I need.

The universe is a divine economy. It runs by the free interchange that takes place between its elements. I take. I use. I give. What I give, another takes, uses, and gives in his turn. Each part of being has its own gift to make. Nothing that I receive do I give back exactly as I received it. Because I am in it, the universe is more than it was. I enrich it by my gifts.

All of us must give—willingly or reluctantly. And we must give all we have; in the end, life will let us hold nothing back. We have the use of many things—for a moment, as with a breath or a thought; for a year or two, as with a coat or a pair of shoes; for many years, as with a house or an inheritance. But we cannot hold on to anything too long. If we do, we will wish we had let it go. We cannot hold on to breath. We cannot hold on to time. Mice and mold spoil the grain kept too long in the granary. The most cleverly hidden gold—the treasure in the tombs of Egypt and China—in time falls into the hands of robbers or is forgotten by all and returns for a season into the bosom of the earth.

This is the parable of the talents. When we merely try to hold on to what is given us, life may take away even that. But when we use what life has given us, when we in our turn give freely, then we may hear the voice of the Master of life, saying, "Well done."

"Give, and it will be given"

Life seeks to give itself. Aeons of evolution culminate in every sprouting seed and would sweep further on. Every living creature is the product of perfection's hungering to bring forth a perfect thing, and all the forces of heaven and earth converge around it and offer themselves to bring it to fulfillment.

The universe holds nothing back. Atom and sun offer their fire. Truths imagination has not dreamed of trip over themselves, trying to make us see them, hoping to be found and used. Powers that would stagger reason lie pent in every crack of space and coil of mind, eager to come forth and do our bidding. Blessings wait everywhere, hungering to bestow themselves, to reshape life and the world, to enable us to surpass all we have ever done or been.

The universe holds nothing back.

Why then do so few of us reach out and partake? Why are there so few George Washington Carvers? Edisons? Einsteins? The music of life gushes forth continually. Why do so few Mozarts ever seem to hear?

Is it that we believe that all things must be earned by sweat and tears?

Is it that we believe that life is meant to be hard and full of suffering?

Is it that we do not believe in the good will of God?

Truth beats at the gates of our mind, but we will not let it in.

Love offers itself in love, and we demand, "What is your price?"

We will not accept our good, though it reaches out to us.

120

"I am unworthy. I am inadequate," we cry.

We insist that life be miserly when it would be only spend-thrift with us. Life loves to be spendthrift. It weighs the vine till it sags and bends the tree to the ground with fruit. It crams the meadows with daisies. It spills song out of the bird. And it beats at our brain with ideas, like rain against a window.

Life cries, "Yet more! Yet more!"

Life gives itself as the sun gives itself, with no thought of holding back. The sun has no thought of making its light hard for us to have.

Life gives itself as a flower gives itself. Effortlessly, easily, in its own perfect time, a flower opens its petals.

Life gives itself as rain gives itself. Rain does not ask of one, "Are you worthy?" or of another, "Have you the price?"

Life gives.

Life gives abundantly.

"I came that they may have life, and have it abundantly," said the Master of life.

And He lived abundantly, naturally, effortlessly, as it is right for one to live who is part of the great economy of nature, infinity's beloved child. For He knew that He had only to give what was His to give, and all the treasures of the universe would be opened up to Him. He knew that He was one with the One, and therefore one with the all. And the One-in-all would gather its powers to feed and care for Him—sending ravens, if need be, as it sent ravens to Elijah. He was a great giver, and He knew that life is the great giving.

"Give, and it will be given," cries the Lord of life, "pressed down, shaken together, running over."

Not pay, and you shall be paid.

Not suffer, and you shall be suffered.

Not labor, and you shall be recompensed for your labor.

Everywhere we look we see life giving itself. We hear it telling us that it is meant to be a giving. It is not meant to be hard and painful. It is meant to be natural and easy.

We have our part to fill, but it is not a hard part. We do not have to pay in pain for the good life lavishes on us. We pay by giving in our turn our own gift.

The universe gives

Life never asks payment for anything. Life gives. We only have to pay when we refuse to give.

This is the great lesson of nature. All things offer themselves. The water does not shrink from our lips, nor the light from our eyes, nor the air from our throats, crying, "Suffer for me. Labor for me. Pay for me."

The earth gives. The sun gives. The universe gives. The furthest stars rain down their light and ask but that we lift our eyes and look up through the dark to take in the golden glory.

Consider how the beauty of God pours out of the great artists. Because they labor over every word? Because they rewrite every phrase of music? Because they rub out and repeat the brush stroke ten thousand times?

Ah, no! Poetry gushed out of Shakespeare. Music cascaded out of Mozart. Michelangelo filled walls, ceilings, canvases with his masterpieces, carved stone and molded metal.

The great Sung painters of China, masters of Zen, painted

pictures as beautiful as men have ever painted. It is told of one of them that after a long productive life he painted a landscape so perfectly that he then stepped into it and vanished from human view.

Yet these men worked on silk with brushes, so it was impossible to erase a single stroke! They gave themselves to their subject. Then, as freely, easily, and spontaneously as life forms a cloud or a sunset or a daisy, they fashioned their painting.

Love does not exact pain payment. Love does not give so that it may receive. Love does not ask to be returned. Love does not offer terms. Love gives because its nature is to give.

God is love. God does not say, "You must do thus and so. Then I will love you."

Does the spring rain say to the seed in the ground, "You must do thus and so, then I will let you grow"?

God is not a keeper of accounts. God is the Giver of good.

The most important things you have were not earned. They are gifts.

Your body is a gift.

Your mind is a gift.

Your capacity for life, thought, feeling, and action is a gift.

Your children are a gift.

Do you have talents? The other name for talent is gift.

Youth is a gift.

Long life is a gift.

Let us then give as we have received. Life will always strike the balance in our favor. If we give as freely as we are able, we will never give back more than a fraction of what we receive. But that is the way life would have it. We are life's beloved children. It gives to us as we give to our children and to those we love.

Nothing in life says, "Pay!" But the whole universe thunders by its example, "Give!" What a world of difference between these words! So long as we think in terms of payment, the world is a drab place where we labor for hire. It is a countinghouse, not the palace of a king. It is a slave compound, not the house of the sons of God. But we only have to labor for hire when we do not give ourselves in love.

The law of the countinghouse is: Work, and you will be paid. But love and life whisper the promise: Give, and it shall be given. How different life would be if we were not to labor grudgingly but to give willingly.

The river at his root

"Lord, make of me a productive channel."

If I could make but a single prayer, it would be this.

It is not that I would not have money and fame and happiness and health and many other things, but above them all I would be a working part of being.

Many of us want to be a star, but we do not want to give any light. But what makes a star a star? A star is a star only because it gives so much light.

Every person knows in his heart—even if he himself cannot live by what he knows—that we live to our utmost when we give to our utmost. It is those who give the most who live the best. Such are the heroes and the geniuses and the saints.

And because what I have to give is not a perfect gift, shall I refuse to give at all?

If what I am able to produce is perfect, that is good. And if what I am able to produce is not perfect, that, too, is good. I shall have given the world what I had to give—the gift of myself.

God is no respecter of persons. We do not have to be perfect or great or good for God to use us. We have only to want to give.

I would reach even to the hand of God and put myself into His hand, so that I might give not only what is in me to give, but what life would give through me.

For the artist is but a hollow reed until the Singer shapes him to His hand. But in the hand of the Singer, what songs will the flute not utter?

Lincoln failed at almost everything he tried. Joan of Arc was an ignorant peasant girl. Mohammed was an illiterate caravan guide. Jesus was a carpenter's son.

But all these learned the true art of giving. They gave not out of the poverty of themselves, but out of the riches of God.

This is to give as a well gives. A well is little in itself but taps the deep and hidden rivers under the earth. A human being is more than a well. God Himself is the river at his root.

Give, and it shall be given—not out of the littleness of self, but out of the largeness and largess of the Lord of life.

Of eating and drinking

The central Christian rite is the mass, a rite of eating and drinking. The officiant prepares bread and wine mixed with water at a table, and the communicants eat the bread and drink the wine—the bread is the body of God and the wine is the blood of God.

Is this not the tremendous and mysterious truth? Is not the act of eating and drinking the act by which—above all else—we enter into the Life Process? We partake; we acknowledge; we assimilate; and we are assimilated by Life. It is given to us, and we give.

All life, including our own, is part of a mystery and a process and does not belong to us but to God. Every meal is a divine meal. Let us not sit down to eat without saying grace.

Each has to give in his turn that which is his to give. The ox has his body to give, and the wheat its grain, and the apple tree its apple. And it is this—their body, their grain, their fruit—that makes them part of the process. We are not kind by refusing to take their gift; we are just excluding them from the economy, from the life process; when we quit eating apples, we will quit planting apple trees.

The ox does not give willingly, but for that matter men often give unwillingly too. In fact, even the greatest of men prayed, "Father . . . remove this cup from me." But nothing survives for long that does not contribute to the process.

The apple tree finds meaning and fulfillment only when the ripe apple drops from the bough or is borne away in a hungry hand.

Do I find meaning and fulfillment in some lesser way?

We are not splinter people

This is a world where nothing lives but something dies.

"Life is suffering," cried the Buddha, and the fathers of

the Christian church echoed his thought with their teaching that this life is a vale of sorrow and man a miserable sinner.

Many spiritual teachers have taught and practiced withdrawal from life. Take no more part in life than you have to, they tell us. Mortify your senses until you have no attachment to anything. Eat as little as possible. Discipline your thoughts until you can stop thinking.

But is this the spiritual way of life?

So one hair of my head might decide that it would have no part of me. And it might detach itself and fall to the earth. But would this profit the hair? or me? or life?

We are not splinter people, fragments, little isolated pieces of life that can find meaning by ourselves, any more than a hair can find meaning by detaching itself from my head or a leaf can find meaning by detaching itself from a tree.

We are part of a process, the life process.

Of ourselves we have no meaning. We find our meaning only by making ourselves part of the process, by letting ourselves be used—and we let ourselves be used by giving what we have to give.

Certainly there is suffering. Perhaps no living thing escapes it altogether. But to withdraw from the life process—is this the way to withdraw from the suffering?

Because one morning the sun is not shining, shall we put out our eyes—or shall we work to invent a light?

There are two ways to meet suffering. One is by withdrawal. The other is by bestowal. We can work to better ourselves. Or we can work to better the world—we can give.

Does not the whole world teach us that nothing lives to itself alone? Nothing exists of itself. Nothing survives of itself.

If the ox and grain withdrew themselves, you would live only a few weeks. If water withdrew itself, you would live only a few days. If air withdrew itself, you would live only a few minutes. If God withdrew Himself, you would not live at all.

If ox and grain and water and air and God cannot withdraw themselves, what right have you to withdraw yourself?

Life demands life. Your life. All your life. But you give your life not by dying, but by living.

How much more a human being gives by living than by dying!

It is by giving our life in living that we make the sum complete, not by taking our life away in dying.

For the ox has his body to give, but man has his mind and spirit.

In the end we shall give our body too—and we shall probably see it go as unwillingly as does the ox. But our body is only a small part of our gift.

Man's gift is to make the world a better place for ox and man.

That the greater may come forth

This is a world where nothing lives but something dies. But it is also a world where nothing dies but something lives!

It is a world of giving.

The seed dies that the tree may live—the seed must expend itself utterly.

The child dies that the adult may live—the child must cease, must give up all its childish ways.

And I really believe that I die so that I may live—more

fully! I the seed. I the child.

Nothing dies but that more life may spring out of it. Always more life!

Did the dinosaur die? Did the saber-toothed tiger die? Did Neanderthal man die?

And did they die that life might be less—or more!

It is only by dying to the lesser that the greater lives.

This is true in myself—and this is true for myself.

Darkness must die so that light may live.

Self-centeredness must die so that selflessness may live.

The littleness that is me must die so that the greatness that I am may come forth.

I do not die because it is a law of life, but only so that the life process may go on.

I die because I do not know how to live. I die because I do not know how to keep on changing and growing—and to change and grow is to live.

I might stand still—but life will not let me.

The human race might stand still—but life will not let it.

Has the wheel turned, and are you at the top of the turn?

And would you stay there forever?

The wheel will turn and make its full turn—but always farther on.

What kind of a world would it be if all things lived on forever—as we now are!

Ahead of the world I see infinite possibilities, and ahead of me I see infinite possibilities.

Now I am as a child—and I would be as a man.

But to be that man I must change and grow.

And to make that change and growth I must slough off this littleness of me, as in the spring a snake sloughs off his last year's skin.

I must be born and born again—and again and again—into a fullness of life that I cannot even imagine. I can only say that I know it is before me—and before you too.

I believe that I will grow some day to the place where I know how to live without death—and without dying.

What kind of life will I have then? I do not know. Perhaps such a life as the sun has, living but without taking life, giving with no thought of return, feeding on its own life-giving powers.

Not by dying, but by love

The gods, I have read, drink nectar and eat ambrosia each morning from the hands of Eternal Youth. I have wondered in what meadow this food grew, and from what vine this juice was pressed. This grape, this grain must give themselves. For immortals could not eat and drink of death, but only of life.

And what gives itself but love? This food and drink of immortality—whose body and whose blood is this if it be not Love's?

For this I know, that the world is now and always has been fed, not by dying, but by love.

When we love, we go bedecked with garlands as to a love feast spread upon an altar table. Love is the bread we eat and the wine we drink—and we are ourselves the bread and the wine of love.

Love does not hold back. Love does not keep itself for

fear. Love does not save itself from want. Love hurries to give itself to all. Love cries to the hungry, "Eat," and to the thirsty, "Drink."

Yet this is the mystery of love—that the more it gives, the more it has to give. When it has given all, it has all to give.

Will it be meaningless to speak of life and death as if these were two separate things, when we grow to the place where all the time we give all that we have to give? When we give all that we have to give, what then will be taken from us? What will be left to die?

And is this not what Love is saying to us from its Cross, where the God who is Love has not died, but has risen into higher life: That he who dies to self lives for love, and he who lives for love never dies!

the achievement of joy

SIX

Life is a dance

The Hindus think of life as a dance. The god wakes, rises, dances, tires of the dance, lies down to sleep again, until once more he wakes, rises, and begins to dance again.

Life is a dance. But it is a dance of life. It is not just a drumming of events, one after another, up and down, back and forth and back again, upon the same stage forever.

Life is movement, growth.

It has times of quiet, but it is a winter quiet, a time of gathering strength to move and flow again in spring.

Life is always an unknown way.

If life invites you, put your hand in God's and go.

Do not hesitate to lead the grand march. For you will dance the dance—make no mistake as to that—though you only tag along at the tail.

If you lead the march, you may set the pace and even decide if the turn will be to the left or right.

Whether you go in the van or in the rear of life, you are going to go.

Earth, solar system, Milky Way, universe—the worlds roar across the trackless deep of space at speeds we cannot even dream.

They race from destiny to destiny, from divine appointment to divine appointment.

Whether we go boldly, laughing and serene, or cower far back in the press, we make the journey with them.

Go then as if you were the principal guest, decked in your fairest raiment, wreathed in flowers; for you have come to the dance—and dance you must.

You can press forward—or be pushed forward.

You can enter boldly in—or be driven blindly in by the press of those who crowd behind you for their place.

You can give—or it will be taken away from you.

Give, then—and live!

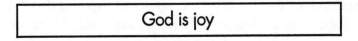

God is joy

We might all be more truly religious if like David we sometimes danced before the Lord and sang Him happy songs.

Often we think of God as love or intelligence or power or life. But how rarely we think of God as joy! Yet think what the world would be like without joy in it. It is only the joy of love that makes us want to be loving and the joy in intelligence that makes us want to know. It is the joy of power that gives us the will to do and the joy in life that gives us the will to live.

Most of the time religion is a solemn affair, and we think of God as immutable law and implacable lawgiver, awesome and absolute. But God is infinite, and the infinite includes the joyous aspects of being.

God is not a god of sorrows. God is the joyous One. It is a kind of blasphemy to think of God as sorrowful. God is the very Spirit of Joy, pouring forth joyousness. The world was formed out of joy. God's joy overflowed, and the world was formed out of its overflowing.

Sadness could never have conceived life. Life—this everlasting bubbling up, this never-ceasing springing forth, this prodigality of creatures, this fantastic exuberance of shapes and forms, this excess of inventions and surprises—could be only the product of a Spirit of Joy. At the heart of things, there is a flame, a dancing flame, a singing flame, a soaring flame, and at it we can warm our hearts.

As a root to water

There are sadness and trouble. But underneath the trouble, working through all, there is the urge toward joy! It is this that gives even the trouble meaning; it is because we sense the joy which might be that we are so troubled. Sorrow is our sense of dissatisfaction with things as they appear. We are dissatisfied because we sense that they might be otherwise.

Some religions have taught the denial of joy. They have felt that life is so full of suffering that the course of wisdom is to shut out all feeling. Or they have taught that God wills suffering, that by suffering here we earn heaven hereafter.

But the human spirit turns as naturally to joy as a root to water or a leaf to light. If we are not joyful, we feel instinctively that something is wrong. Joy is not only right for our own sake, we owe it to others, we owe it to God. We should never deny a joy except for a greater joy, our own or another's.

Life is the good work of a good God, a God who meant us for good, who meant life for good, who meant the world for good. God does not require that every joy be paid for by a sorrow. What kind of a God would dole out joy at such a rate?

Joy does not come out of sorrow, or sorrow out of joy. Does hate come out of love or ignorance out of knowledge? Joy comes out of a joyful spirit, as water out of a spring.

We need not accept

Because we are a part of life, we have the experiences that are part of life. Some of these are easy, some of them hard. But the easy experiences we can meet rejoicing, and the hard we can meet triumphant. For it is our nature as dreamers and builders, as God's children, that we need not accept things as they are but can change them into something better. And this we are constantly striving to do: to turn the wilderness into a garden, to make the desert bloom, to build dikes against the sea, to change poverty into riches, sickness into health, war into peace, death into life; to remake ourselves and the world nearer to the heart's desire, the heart of love whose infinite compassion encompasses all things.

This is the great condition of our being; that we need not settle for pain, for poverty, for limitation, for death! We may settle for them, but we do not have to. And always, here and there, the true heroes of the race are refusing to settle for them, illumining some area of ignorance, making poverty retreat another step, forcing sickness to give up its domain, rolling death a little further back, making chaos yield to order, making the lesser change for the greater, making the old give way to the new, winning the victory for life, for joy, for God!

We are alive, the children of life. We have hands and a heart and the power of thought! We are not molded by things, things are molded by us. The stuff of the universe is ours to grasp and shape and change.

Our advances are not paid for by retreats. As with a mountain climber, the highest point we reach becomes the base camp from which we start our next attempt until at last we scale the peak. This is the whole history of the human race, the whole story of life.

There will be hills to climb, but God has given us the kind of heart that is not daunted by hills. God has given us a hilltop heart.

Even when we cannot play the notes

It is not when life asks least of us that we get the most from living, but when life asks most of us, when life makes the greatest demands on us. We are nearer akin to the tree that grapples at timberline with rocks and winds and sun and frost than to the hothouse orchid.

Life is joyous. It may or may not be easy. It may be hard in the sense that writing a poem or building a house or running a four-minute mile is hard.

Comfort may be joy, but joy is also discomfort. Runners in a race, their breath like a flame, may be at the full stride of joy. The men who climbed Mount Everest, hungry, weary, panting, frozen—were they not at the peak of joy? After that summit, what will not look like plains—unless they discover the Himalayas of the heart and mind that rise infinitely higher and are harder yet to climb?

The gardener—spading, tilling, planting, weeding, watering, tending, wrestling with reluctant soil—has found joy.

The composer—working for weeks on a single passage of his symphony, giving up food, companionship, sleep—has found joy.

For joy comes from being what we were born to be. This is the whole secret of joy: being that which we were born to be, doing that which we were made to do.

We can be happy or unhappy with or without things. There is no assurance of joy in gaining things or in giving

139

them up. A banker may be happy or unhappy. So may a monk. Not what we have, but what we are—this is the measure of our happiness. To be less than what we might have been is to fall short of the joy we might have had. There is no goal worth stopping at except the goal of the whole person. The whole person is threefold—body, mind, and spirit.

In the course of life we may experience pain, but that does not mean that the good will of God or the good way of life is pain. We are like children learning to play the song of life. Now we may stumble over hard passages, but the song the Composer has written is a joyous, triumphant song. It is not an easy song, but it is a beautiful song. It is the song of the sons and daughters of God! And this is the true art of living: to hear the song God has written even when we cannot play the notes.

The posture of joy

Some feel that joy is shallow. But if there be a bliss of ignorance, there is a bliss of comprehension too, a deep joy given only to those who see deeply into the meaning of things, so deeply that they reach the eternal truth at the core of changing facts and see that nothing is meaningless, and that the meaning is good.

Joy is an achievement; not a gift, but earned. Joy shows the mettle of the mind. The joyful ones are usually not those who have had little to meet, but those who have met much.

Joy is the sign not of shallow thinking, but of a deep faith. Anyone can give way to despair, but only those who have faith in life and love for life keep going when the way grows hard. Not those who resign themselves to sadness but those who keep faith in the good and continue to expect the good, in the face of what looks like certain failure and defeat, are those who win joy—for themselves and for humankind. The small boy whistling in the dark and keeping on his way is a symbol of the whole human race.

The spirit to whistle when we do not feel like whistling, the heart to sing when we do not feel like a song, the faith to affirm the goodness of God when we see no facts to justify our affirmation—from these has the greatness of human-kind sprung, with these have the victories of life been won.

It is not the dour and downhearted who are best able to bear pain if it comes, but the happy-hearted. These make the best of pain as they make the most of pleasure.

A happy heart may not assure you that you will have noth-ing to meet, but it does assure you of a happy heart with which to meet it. And a happy heart will bear time's strains, as a dancing spring of steel will bear strains that will break the stoutest rod.

You can have the habit of a happy heart.

Happiness is a habit, as unhappiness is a habit.

Would you be joyous? Assume the posture of joy.

Assume the posture of sorrow, and soon you begin to feel sorrowful. Act joyful, and you begin to feel that all is well. Sorrow is a recumbent figure, immobile and supine. But joy will not lie still. Joy is dancing thoughts. Joy stands tiptoe at the top of the heart. Joy bounds for joyousness. Joy rushes to meet the object of its joy. Joy is action.

Would you be joyous? Be active. Put all you are into all you do. Live with the whole of you. Is the moment a great victory that you have dreamed of and labored for? Savor it. Is the moment a bit of passing sweet? Savor it no less.

Love is joy

If you give little of yourself, you will get little joy.

The vessel you hold up to life, life fills. Hold up half a cup, and you will receive half a portion.

And how more can you give yourself to life than by love? To love is to live with the whole of you, for to love is to give yourself to what you love.

A grandmother came to the Buddha weeping for her dead grandson. "Would you like to have as many grandchildren as there are people in the city?" he asked. "Yes, yes!" she cried. "But then you would have to weep every day," he said, "for in the city people die daily. Those who have a hundred loved ones have a hundred woes; those who have ten loved ones have ten woes; those who have one loved one have one woe; those who have no loved one have no woe."

But He who gave Himself to all said, "Love!" The answer to sorrow is not less love, but more. Such is the mystery of love. If you could love ten thousand, you would suffer not ten thousand times more but ten thousand times less. Love none, and your whole life is woe. Love all, and there is no room for anything else but love—and love is joy.

When you say yea to one joy, do you say yea to all woe? Perhaps, but you are also saying yea to all joy!

Life is a river. Try to grasp it in your fingers, and it spurts through your fingers. Try to dam it up, and it overflows your dam. But give yourself to life, as a waterwheel gives itself to the river, and you will find that life and the joy of life give themselves to you.

Surely the highest joy is this: to do not your will, but the will of the Lord of your being, taking from life what there is to take, giving to life what you have to give, doing what you have power to do, being what you were meant to be; not a little, lonely, frightened, separate, aching self, but used by the joyous One for the joyousness of all. To do this is to find joy in all seasons and circumstances, in the giving and the receiving, in the withholding and the pouring forth. To do this is to live each moment to the fullness of joy, yet to have forever; to be part of the infinite, yet to bring the self to a joyous flowering!

perfect world—perfect man
SEVEN

A vision of perfection

One day when I was talking with God, I said: "Dear God, why did You make the world as You made it? You are perfect Intelligence and perfect Love. Why did You make the world the way it is instead of the way it might have been?"

So God said to me, "Look."

Then I had a vision of the world as perfect.

I looked and saw it radiant and complete.

The perfect galaxies circled in perfect glory through perfect absolutes of emptiness.

The perfect sun shone in the perfect sky. The perfect birds soared in the perfect air. The perfect lamb played with the perfect lion. The perfect trees gave of their perfect fruit. And in all the perfect cities there was only the perfect activity of perfect beings.

I saw infinity immaculate and orderly, perfect beyond all praising, and I saw it consummately full of perfect things.

Then I saw that I was running. As hard as I could run, I ran around and around that perfect world. But nowhere in all its glittering perfection could I find what I was searching for.

At last I could not bear to search any longer. I fell down and hid my eyes in my hands, and I cried out, "But dear God, where am I?"

Again God said, "Look."

I looked and saw I was in my own room. Around me were my soiled, familiar daily things—the ruffled carpet, the scarred desk, the papers not too neatly sorted out. Through the window where the curtain hung somewhat awry, I could see the bare branches of the tree blowing in the sometime wind.

"But God," I said, "this is my usual world."

"It is the world," said God, "as I have made it to make you in it. Tell me, please, what world is better than that?"

The perfect seed

God made us the perfect seed.

He did not make us the perfect tree, but the perfect seed. He did not make us as we might have been, but as we might become.

Part of the goodness of what He made is the fact that it is becoming—it is not finished.

We are not yet there.

He made us the good start—He did not make us already across the line. He made the good race beginning, not ended.

How good a life would it have been had He made it already over?

He made life good, not finished.

He made life perfect, not perfected.

There is a tremendous and important difference.

The perfect butterfly is for a time a perfect caterpillar. It is no less perfect when it is a caterpillar than when it is a butterfly. In fact, if it is not a perfect caterpillar, it will never be a perfect butterfly.

The perfect lily is a withered, brown bulb.

The perfect maple is a green-winged seed.

The perfect rose is a thorny stub in the ground.

When we think of perfection, we can think of two kinds of

worlds.

One is static. We can only say of it, "It is." It is complete. It is perfect. It is permanent. It is unchanging. It is whole.

This is the kind of world we ordinarily think of when we think of heaven—we arrive in it with our life already finished and complete, and there we are. When we try to think of what we are going to do there, we can only think of sitting on a cloud and playing a harp. There is nothing to do because everything is already done; everything has been perfected.

This heaven is a perfect world. But it is perfection for the dead—and that is what we imagine it for. It is inert perfection, and it is for inert things.

There is another kind of perfect world. It is a world that is perfectly alive. In it there is no finished perfection. There is only perfection begun.

This world contains hopes, potentialities, limitless possibilities. In this world nothing is done. Everything is to do.

This is the kind of world life has made for us.

Life is a journey, but the journey is not over—it is only begun.

Suppose God said to you, "I am going to give you a trip around the world."

You said, "Thank you, God."

He said, "How did you like it?"

You said, "But I have not even begun."

He said, "Oh yes, I gave you the trip complete and completed. Look back and you will see what a perfect trip it was. You have had an absolutely perfect trip around the world."

I think you would feel cheated. I think you would feel you had never had a trip.

The joy of a journey

The joy of a journey is not in having arrived. The joy is in the journeying. It is as much in the first step as in the last step. A journey that you had complete, the last step with the first, arrival with departure—this is no living journey for living creatures.

Living perfection, perfection for living, perfect living has to contain challenges, incidents, surprises, changes—unknowns as well as knowns.

It is a great and high thing to be alive.

God made life to grow.

It is only when it is growing that life is perfect. When life stops growing, life is not alive. Halt the wave even at the crest, and it is no longer a wave.

To be a human being is a great thing, a high thing too.

And God made us to grow.

To grow is not easy. It is a natural thing, but a hard thing.

Yet it is only by doing this hard thing—by growing—that we are perfect.

A perfect statue of a human being is finished. Flawless in every detail, right in every proportion. We may stand and gape at it in admiration, even envy.

But a perfect statue is a stone.

Perfect Man is something else again. Reaching higher than he can grasp, aiming farther than he can hit, envisioning more than he can embody, never as much as he might become, yet more than he might have been—Perfect Man is perfectly alive.

What do I mean when I say Perfect Man? I mean the

embodiment of the human potential at its highest peak of possibility. I do not mean a man more than a woman. They must both become that which they are capable of becoming. They must grow to be that which they are meant to be, that which God had in mind before He made Adam and Eve and brought them forth to take "dominion over the fish of the sea, and over the birds of the air . . . and over every creeping thing that creeps upon the earth" . . . and most of all, over themselves.

Which would you rather be—Michelangelo's *David* flawless in the square at Florence, or a newborn child?

One of the greatest of all Chinese writers was a man named Chuang-tze who lived about three hundred years before Christ.

One day when he was fishing, an official approached him and asked him to become a state administrator.

Chuang-tze, continuing to fish, said, "I have heard that in the city there is a sacred tortoise which has been dead now some three thousand years. The prince keeps him perfectly preserved in a beautiful chest on the temple altar. Now would this tortoise rather be dead and venerated or alive and wagging its tail in the mud?"

"Alive," said the official, "and wagging its tail in the mud."

"Begone!" said Chuang-tze. "I, too, will wag my tail in the mud!"

A world so good

God did not make a world of pain or fear or hate.

God made a world so good that it is possible for you and me to be in it.

God made a world so good that it is possible for God to be in it.

God made a world so good that it has Godlike possibilities.

God did not make a world where we get everything we wish for. But would this have been a perfect world? It would have been a world of unimaginable disorder.

God did make a world that is an orderly world. This is a world where every seed brings forth after its kind. This is as true for the seeds we plant in our mind as for the seeds we plant in the earth. Every desire, every thought, every word, every act is a seed; if we water and feed and cultivate and care for it, it will bring forth after its kind—noxious weed if we have planted noxious weed, fruiting tree if we have planted fruiting tree.

Perfection is not a static state. Perfection is alive. Perfection is the maximum life. It is not the finished product. It is the living process.

Perfection for a living universe is as different as you can conceive from perfection in a static universe. I am most alive when I am least static. I am most alive when I am growing most.

The perfect world for living things is the world in which they are growing.

I am not a clay pot shaped by a potter, perfect only when he sets me glazed and beautiful on the shelf of heaven for eternity to gaze at.

Perfection for me is growth.

To be perfect is to be growing.

To be perfect is to be moving in a divine direction.

For things alive, goodness is not a *state* of goodness. It is *living* goodness. It is growing goodness. It contains the possibility of evil, because only by rejecting evil can living things be good!

Can the good world for the fish be less than the ocean, with its limitless perils and potentialities?

Can the good world for the bird be less than the sky, with its winds and wideness, its hawks and storms?

Can the good world for the tree be less than wind and rain, sun and storm, drought and flood, even woodcutters?

And can we think that the good world for us would be a lesser world than the world of trees and birds and fishes?

Not a one-note world

Consider music. The dominant seventh is a dissonance. The tonic chord is a consonance. But imagine a piece of music that was all tonic chords. We like it when the music rests for a moment on the tonic chord, but how weary it would become if it stayed there.

Life is like music.

It is not one note, but many.

One note can never be goodness in music, no matter how perfect the note may be.

One moment can never be goodness in life, no matter how enjoyable the moment may be.

You are music—not a little piping, one-note, perfect piece, but a swelling symphony of life and power, endlessly, endlessly, endlessly growing in sweep and beauty and joyous expression—and your world is not a one-note world. It is a music hall fitting for God's music to be played in it.

Astronomers tell us the universe is expanding. They speak

of the red shift and of worlds rushing out, out, out away from one another across billions of light-years.

Of course, we live in a universe that is expanding. We live in a growing universe, for it is a living universe.

What other kind of universe would we expect the living God to make for life to live in!

The world is growing. The bud of the world uncurls, and at its tip yet further worlds are born, unfold in twig and leaf, stretch forth, expand and grow, and put forth curling buds of worlds again.

God made us the perfect seed.

And He made the world the kind of world in which His seed would grow.

What would you have me be?

We are more a journey than a destination.

Not by reaching an end do we fulfill ourselves, but by reaching toward an end—and an end is always a new beginning.

Life is growth.

I am to grow. You are to grow. The whole of things is to grow.

What are you?

You are to be yet more.

The rose must be the perfect rose.

Man must be Perfect Man.

And when man has become Perfect Man, what then?

Then, when that which is Less-than-Man has ceased to be,

that which is More-than-Man will have begun to appear.

There is always one more step.

Hills always have another side.

When you have gone as far as you can go, you will see a new direction in which you can strike out.

There is a pattern in us that we strive to fashion ourselves after.

We may not be conscious of the pattern.

Does the acorn have foreknowledge of the oak?

Or the nympha of the dragonfly?

Or the single cell in my mother's womb of me?

But the pattern is there. And it shapes and spurs us on.

It is the human seed of God.

It breaks through the husks.

It alters and transforms itself.

It grows.

And I cry out, "O human seed of God, shaping me and changing me, goading me to be this only to make me want to be that, prodding me always to be striving to surpass myself, leaving me unsatisfied no matter what I become, what would you have me be?"

And the answer comes even in the asking—in the reaching to be yet more.

What would you like to be like?

What is your idea of Perfect Man?

What would you like to be like? What would you like all

people to be like?

Is your Perfect Man the mendicant saint seated in silent meditation?

Or the barefoot monk giving his life to help the poor and sick and dispossessed?

Or the general-king leading victorious armies to conquest?

Or the artist in a garret catching a vision of beauty?

Or the great thinker exploring the unknown?

Or the scientist laboring in a laboratory to uncover new truths about the universe?

Or the rich man?

Or the great lover?

Or the handsome athlete?

Perhaps you would want your Perfect Man to have a little of all—to have intelligence like an Einstein or an Aristotle; courage like a Siegfried or King Arthur; selflessness like a St. Francis or the Buddha; mastering ability like a Henry Ford or a Napoleon; good sense like a Confucius; strength like a Jack Dempsey or a Jesse Owens; vigor like a Goethe or a Churchill; inspiration like a Michelangelo or a Shakespeare.

Or if you are a woman, who is your ideal of womanhood? Queen Elizabeth? Marie Curie? Joan of Arc? Esther? Brunnehilde? Rosa Parks?

To many people the figure of Perfect Man is not a man but a woman—the Great Mother. You may know her as Kali or Kwanyin or Mary, or by any of a hundred names.

In the myth, Paris had to choose Perfect Woman. Hera, the wife of Zeus; Diana, the virgin huntress; and Aphrodite, the mistress of love, came to him. He chose love and brought on the Trojan War.

I imagine most of us in the Western World, when

choosing Perfect Man, would choose Jesus.

His face looks down at us from innumerable walls—not the face of an individual, for no one knows what the historical Jesus looked like, but the face of Perfect Man, as each artist has envisioned Him.

And the story, as it has come down to us, is it meaningful because it is historical fact—or because it is the story of Perfect Man?

On a Friday morning

On a Friday morning—according to the story—they condemned the Man to death. They nailed Him to the Cross, and there He died. When He was dead, they buried Him. Across the opening of the tomb, they rolled a stone.

But on Sunday morning, a friend of His—a woman named Mary Magdalene, who had come to grieve at His graveside—found the stone rolled away and the tomb empty. She ran toward a man she took to be the gardener.

The man said, "Woman, why weepest thou?"

She, turning and looking at Him, recognized the risen Christ!

Since then, the world has debated this wonder. Did Jesus really rise from the dead?

But the wonder is not that He rose.

The wonder is that the world could believe it might have kept Him in the tomb.

Four hundred years before Jesus, another man stood before his judges in another place. His accusers said he was an atheist because he had taught their sons to think and to question the accepted prejudices of the times.

This man said many beautiful and moving things that afternoon. Among other things, he said:

"Nothing will injure me, not Meletus nor Anytus [two of his accusers]—they cannot, for a bad man is not permitted to injure a better than himself. I do not deny that Anytus may, perhaps, kill me . . . and he may imagine, and others may imagine, that he is inflicting a great injury upon me: but there I do not agree."

Anytus and the other Athenians found Socrates guilty that afternoon, and a short time later he drank the hemlock and died.

But they could not keep Socrates in the tomb either. As I write this, I put down my pencil and turn and read again of his trial and death. And like Plato and Crito and Cebes and Simnias and all his other friends who watched that afternoon, I weep too. So that once more—across the ages, but undimmed by time—the clear, calm voice must come:

"What is this strange outcry? I sent away the women mainly in order that they might not offend in this way. . . . Be quiet then and have patience."

The world sits in puzzlement over the resurrection of Jesus. The world sits in puzzlement over a statement like that made by Socrates: "You may kill me, but you cannot injure me."

Such things do not make sense—to the world.

And I suppose we all at first have to take such statements as Socrates' that nothing, not even death, can injure him, and such acts as Jesus' rising from the dead, on faith.

We have to believe them to be true.

But we believe such things, not blindly but because something in our nature and the nature of life, as we observe it, gives evidence that they are true.

The truth is that the world cannot keep truth in the tomb. Not any truth. Not the least truth. It never has been able to. It never will be able to.

The world cannot keep beauty in the tomb. The world cannot keep life in the tomb. The world cannot keep good in the tomb. The world cannot keep love in the tomb.

The world has mocked, stoned, scourged, poisoned, crucified, hanged, burned, and set truth before its firing squads. It has buried truth and turned away, washing its hands in relief that it has gotten rid of truth so simply.

But truth has never stayed in the tomb.

Even as they crucified Jesus, He was at work in people's hearts. And He still is!

The wonder is not that Jesus rose. The wonder is that the world was able to keep Him in the tomb even three days.

The story of the resurrection of Jesus is the truest story ever told. It is the essence of truth because it is the essence of life. It would be true even if it had never happened.

Jesus is Perfect Man. He is perfect goodness. He is perfect love. He is perfect faith. He is perfect life.

Different Christians have different notions about how He became Perfect Man. We may believe that He came direct from the throne of heaven and was born of a virgin on a night of miracles. Or we may believe that He had perfected Himself over many lifetimes and through infinite ages—even as you and I must perfect ourselves. Or we may just believe that He was a man of love and a teacher of truth.

But to all of us He is Perfect Man. He is ideal man, and man's ideal of love and goodness. He is the divine Man— God but Man, God as Man, the God-Man. He is Perfect Man, but He is Man. He is the Man we only aspire toward, but He told us that what He did, we shall do also, and greater works than these shall we do.

And He showed that Perfect Man cannot be slain, or, if he die, will live again.

Good shall be victorious

Now, two thousand years away, we still stand at the foot of the hill, at the foot of the Cross, and we watch the man Jesus dying in the afternoon and borne away into the tomb. And we hear Him saying still:

"I am the resurrection, and the life: he that believeth in me, though he were dead, yet shall he live: And whosoever liveth and believeth in me shall never die. Believest thou this?"

We hear Socrates affirming, "You cannot injure a good man."

But Jesus was crucified. Socrates drank the hemlock. Certainly good does not always seem to triumph. Would it not seem, then, that these men were wrong?

But is this not Socrates I hear still calling to me, still alive, more alive than he was that afternoon in ancient Athens? Has he not stirred every generation of men since to seek the truth more diligently? And where now are his accusers?

Is this not Jesus I see, still looking down at me with infinite compassion? Have not these eyes become more surely the eyes of love than they were when they reflected Galilee? Has not every generation since, looking on this gentle face, been lifted nearer to perfection?

These men are offering us a higher reality. They are affirming the victory of good. They are saying that good is at work—no matter what appearances may indicate—for them that work for the good. We may not always see the good, but the good is there; all the evil there is cannot affect it.

All the darkness in the world cannot put out the light of one small candle. But one small candle may light a world or a heart of darkness.

Death is not death

Not the least thing Jesus and Socrates are saying is that death is not death. The hemlock, the Cross are not the end. If there is crucifixion, there is also resurrection. The shadow of the Cross cannot obscure the light of Easter morning.

We can fix our gaze on the death and the dying, on trouble and evil and imperfection. But this is not the whole view. Life is whole, and to be understood, it must be seen whole.

It is not that the facts are not the facts. It is just that they are not the truth. Believing that the facts are the truth is like believing that the sun has stopped shining because we happen at the moment to be in darkness. The long day's journey is not into the night. Though we move through ten thousand nights, the journey is and always has been toward a brighter day.

The setting sun is but the other side of the rising sun. On the other side of the Crucifixion is resurrection.

We cannot see the full circle of the stars forever shining round the Throne of the Ageless—we glimpse them only as they pass before us one by one. Nevertheless, even from this part view, seeing things moment by moment and little by little, we see that if there is darkness, there is also light.

It is as when we climb a mountain. Sometimes to reach the peak we have to go down into a valley. But when we emerge, we are closer to the peak. God gave us a hilltop kind of heart.

Life does not go backward. Life goes forward. Life is like Napoleon's drummer boy. It does not know how to beat retreat. Its bugles, even blowing requiem, sound for the living and are a call to life. When the winding of the horn has died away upon the air and pulses only in our heart, we lift our eyes to green endeavors.

Perfect Man, come forth

Life does not move toward death. It moves toward more life. It turns death into life. It turns inanimate matter into life. It turns lesser forms of life into higher forms of life. It invents. It evolves. It shapes itself into new and ever more various creatures, with greater capacities for living. It moves from brute to human, and from human—! Even now the life-force is seething in us all, pressing to outstrip itself, to surpass and overtop all that it has so far done.

There is brutality. But it is love that is growing. There is ignorance. But it is intelligence that is growing. There is pain. But it is joy and the capacity for joy that is growing. There is resistance. But it is our power for constructive action that is growing. It is not the evil that grows, it is the good.

Along our way stand many crosses, where often we have crucified the best and highest in ourselves. Yet we still keep coming and becoming.

What are we becoming?

Perfect Man.

Perfect Man is in us all.

I do not believe that there is anyone in the world who does not feel this. This is why we all feel uneasy, frustrated, guilty—all feel that we fall short. Because we all feel that we were made for perfection.

But this is also why we long, strive, hope, keep on. This is why we do not let facts or failings keep us from rising up and starting out again.

Because Perfect Man is in us.

Many times we have heard the Perfect Man in us urge us, "Live!" Many times He has invited us, "Love!" Many times He has pressed us to keep faith with Him through some Gethsemane. And many times, for thirty pieces of silver, we have kissed Him and betrayed Him.

But Perfect Man in us says in perfect love, "Though you slay me, yet I shall never die. Though I were dead, yet shall I live."

And there He is again—to trouble us with dreams and longings; to get us not to give up even before what seems to be impossible; to stir us to believe we can do better even when we cannot see how; to give us heart to make yet one try more; always to make us dissatisfied with our lesser self; to let us never settle for less than Perfect Man.

The urge to bring forth Perfect Man beats in us like a winged thing against bars.

But who forged the bars?

Who keeps us there?

We are made for living, not dying.

For rising up.

For going forward.

For truth. For love. For joy.

We are made to be Perfect Man.
And neither cross nor tomb can keep us from our good.
Perfect Man, come forth!
It is resurrection morning.

your own heaven, your own hell

EIGHT

Why do we make God less than we are?

God is not a bookkeeper.

God is not a prison warden.

God is not a grand inquisitor.

People reject capital punishment. They even try to end life imprisonment. They want to help the person who has committed a crime become part of the human community.

Why do we make God less than we are?

I wonder if there is a single intelligent person of our time who believes in Hell—or Heaven—the way our grandparents did—as places where the dead dwell, in pearly bliss or in flames, forever.

Eternal states? Eternal static!

I cannot imagine a God who would condemn His children to eternal pain.

I am no better than I am. I have learned to love only a little. But even I—if I should make a world—I might not make it wisely well, but I would put into it all the love I could. Even I, who love imperfectly, would not make a Hell!

And God is Perfect Love. How far God's world surpasses anything I might make of it! The truth about the world is beyond my farthest imaginings, beyond even my highest hopes. And it is as far beyond the imaginings of you who imagine eternal damnation as love is beyond hate!

There is no sign in nature of a principle that punishes. There is only the sign of a healing power, a righting power. When I break a law, I suffer the consequences. But the law does not punish me, it merely acts to restore the balance, to set things in harmony again, so that I will have not pain, but joy.

167

If I eat the wrong food, my stomach does not curse me or judge me. Its concern is not to punish me; its sole concern is to handle the unwise food as wisely as it can, to set things right for me.

If I cut my finger, my finger does not upbraid me or punish me for my wrongdoing. It just sets out immediately to heal the wound.

Is God inferior to my finger or my stomach?

The universe does not want pain. It wants growth. It is never interested in punishing me; it is interested in my well-being, for my well-being is the well-being of the universe.

As to Heaven

As to Heaven, imagining Heaven is as hard as believing in Hell.

For me to live even another hundred years with any hope of happiness, I would have to have also a power to change and grow infinitely, a power to start anew continually—to live even for a hundred years, not for eternity!

But change and growth are what Heaven and Hell cannot possibly be—by the very terms by which we are condemned to them. They are *eternal* bliss, *eternal* damnation!

We go to them—and there we are, fixed forever! There cannot possibly be changing—certainly not growing in them—or we might grow out of them!

They are perfect states—the perfect best, the perfect worst.

And what we might be there is impossible to imagine because it cannot possibly be what we are here—here we are not perfectly bad or perfectly good.

We are told that in Heaven we will be reunited with our loved ones forever. Try to imagine it.

My babe whom I lost—how will I know him? How will he know me? Will I be the mother he had then—or the person I am now? And he—is he doomed always to infantile bliss, so that I may be the eternal mother with the eternal babe in her arms?

The Zoroastrians from whom we took much of our notion of Heaven and Hell—even the name Paradise—tried to make it make sense by saying that all children would be fifteen there and all adults forty. But fifteen and forty forever—dear children and dear adults, would you, even if you could?

The Zoroastrians, at least, were kinder than we Christians; they said that this static world would not last forever, but only for an age.

For myself, I do not believe in an afterlife that is unchanging for eternity. Unchanging is the one thing life is not.

Life is change. And living people change with life.

We are travelers, and we make a journey. Some walk beside us a long way, others a little while. Some lodge with us for a night in the same inn. But sooner or later we all go our separate roads, for we all have our own way to find, our own work to do, our own growth to make, our own vision to follow—and if we are honest, we would not have it any other way. If somewhere we meet again, those I love will—I am confident—be more than they were when I last saw them. I pray that I may be more too.

If somehow we recognize each other (and I believe we always do), it will not be superficially—by resemblances of face or recollection of past lives and old relationships—but deeply, by bonds of love and common purpose; by mutual attraction of mind and spirit; by a communion that is not of words or even thoughts, but is an inward oneness; by the same spontaneous springing up of recognition that drew us together here, brother with brother, mother with child, husband with wife, and friend with friend, we will be drawn again.

A vision of Hell

Once I had a vision of Hell.

As I was dragged past him down into the pit, I recognized Cerberus, the three-headed dog who guards the entrance, so I knew that it had to be Hell.

But I could not believe it.

I showed such outrage and dismay that the demon who was dragging me was disturbed.

"It is not as bad as you think," he said. "You may not have to stay here long."

"I will stay here long," I said. "I did not believe that God could make a place like this, and I still cannot believe it. The maker of this place has only my hatred and contempt, and he will always have it. He will have to bind me and torture me. For I will fight against him with all my might and strength."

"You have the wrong idea about the place," said the demon, dragging me lower into the pit. "It is not like what you think it is at all. There is nobody here, you see, except those you feel ought to be here. Look around you."

I looked and saw that what the demon said was true. I could see nobody whom I had not thought deserved to be in Hell.

"Hell can only last as long as you feel it should be here,"

the demon said.

The rest of my vision I cannot remember—whether I slunk down yet deeper into that pit of my shame and fear and hate or whether in my unforgiveness I could not let Hell go.

We are our own gatekeepers

I believe in Heaven and Hell—but not as states of arrested development in the world of the dead. They are as much herenow as they are going to be hereafter. They are states in you and me. The gulf between them is no wider than a thought.

Hell is my own heart's crying out for punishment; Heaven my own mind's vision of perfection.

I build Hell out of my shame, my fear, my hate—not God's. So long as I believe there ought to be one—for anybody—so long do I remain there.

And what is Heaven but my awareness of God's presence? When I have this, what more can Heaven be! And shall I put this off to some future time?

Can I believe there is a place where God is not, even Hell?

No, the God I believe in is there as He is here—and God is Love. Where love is, that is Heaven—even if in Hell. Let me have love in my heart—and you can have your hypothetical city in the hereafter.

I know people who spend every day in Heaven and people who spend every day in Hell.

I walk along the street, and I see them passing by. I cannot tell by looking in which world people live. They may wear the same clothes and even the same faces—but sometimes a face is not a face, but a mask.

I cannot tell by listening to their speech. I say, "Good morning," and they say, "Good morning." Sometimes if we talk long enough, I may learn their real condition. But speech often hides more than it reveals.

Most of us do not ourselves know whether we are in Heaven or Hell. We have no standard of judgment. Most of us go through life assuming ours is the normal state and that other people feel just what we feel. My peace against your peace, my joy against your joy, my level of living against your level of living—how shall I measure it? I am myself my only measure. Relativity is just as true in spiritual matters as in matters of space.

We are like children born blind in a kingdom of the blind. We can only interpret light in terms of our blindness.

True saints are hardly ever aware that they are saints. True human goodness is unself-conscious; when it becomes self-conscious, it is not so good. For the most part, saints simply go about doing what is natural for them to do; their world is a world where it seems right for everything to be loved, so they love. They not only give without letting others see them giving; they do not even see themselves as giving. They give as sun and rain give, as grass and trees give; giving is their usual life.

The high gods do not dwell aloof and unconcerned upon some ultimate peak of thought, but in the lowest valley of the soul. For who but the highest can become lower than the lowest? Who but the highest can so humble themselves that even the lost may be moved to pity? Do not look toward Olympus to find the Heaven dwellers; look in the valley of the lost. It is there you will find them doing Heaven's work.

And those who are in Hell, like those who are in Heaven, often do not know that they are there. They are on fire, but they have grown so accustomed to the fire that it seems just the natural condition of life.

Their world is a world full of things that seem right and reasonable to hate and fear. So they go around doing what seems to them to be only right and reasonable.

They do not think of themselves as fearful. They may even be daredevils.

They do not think of themselves as hating. "I love everybody," they may say.

When one day they become aware that they are on fire, they have taken the first step toward putting the fire out.

But the fire burns, whether we are aware of it or not. And only love puts out the fire, whether we are aware of that or not.

If one morning you awoke feeling the way some people feel every morning, you would cry out, "I am in Hell."

And if one morning you awoke feeling the way other people feel every morning, you would cry out, "What a heavenly morning! I have never felt this good before in all my life."

This is Hell. This is Heaven.

At every circle of Hell I think that I might find some human heart, and I might find some human heart at every round of Heaven.

Where I am, there I am.

Where you are, there you are.

But no one keeps us there—except ourselves. We are ourselves the keeper of the gate.

You can never go back

The Hindus tell of different heavens and different hells.

To picture the difference between them, they tell this story:

Imagine the happiest prince in the world. He has just won the world's richest kingdom. He has conquered his deadliest foes in personal combat and put all their armies to flight. He has just wed the world's most beautiful princess. Now he mounts his throne surrounded by his loyal subjects loading him with gifts and shouting his praises.

The happiness of the meanest inhabitant of the next higher level of consciousness is ten thousand times greater than that of this prince.

As we live, we all move from level to level in consciousness. We go up a path, and as we go, things change and we change. Old views disappear; new views open before us.

It is as when we move from city to city. We can never go back. We may think we can go back. We may wish to go back. We may look back with longing and think to ourselves, "Ah, that was the good life then!" We may even go back to what we thought was the city we left. But it will not be there, not the city we remember.

Once you come up a step, you can never go back. It does not take you long to learn that you cannot warm yourself by last night's fire, however brightly it may blaze in your memory. Now it is only a heap of ashes, and if you would be warm, you must build another fire.

Once you have come through the gate, you will not go back again. You may take a step back, you may slip back— but you will not stay there for long.

Once you have run with the foxes, how can you go back to

being a hare again? Better to be the least of foxes than king of the hares.

Once you know what it feels like to be at peace, how long will you be content to live in disorder?

Once you know how to turn on the light, how long will you stay in the dark?

Once you become more, you will never settle for less.

All the happy toys of childhood—the dolls and the lead soldiers—where are they now?

You are what you are

All you who like to condemn men and women to Hell, you sitters in judgment on God and the world, you moralizers, life is not eternal pain and punishment. If your morals make you think so, it is time you changed them.

You have been frightening people in the name of religion for thousands of years—and how many people have been frightened into being good?

Now others like you are frightening people in the name of science—and how many people are being frightened into being good?

People are going to have to be loved into being good. People are going to have to be trusted into being good. This means that we ourselves are going to have to be good. But there is no other way.

Hatred has never put out hatred. Only love puts out hatred; it changes it to love. Fear has never put out fear. Only faith puts out fear; it changes it to faith.

There is no great Judgment Day after death when you are

going to be dragged before God.

You die daily, and every day is Judgment Day. When do you not stand before God?

You are judged right now, and your sentence is branded on your brow. Do not tell me that you do not feel the weight of your shackles?

But who placed them there? And who keeps them there?

You are judged by what you are!

This is all the judgment there is. This is all the judgment there will ever be.

The only punishment or reward in nature—and it is inescapable—is that a person must be what he has become. If brute, brutal! If god, godlike!

What are you?

You are meant to be a human being! You are meant to be all that a human being is capable of being!

And what is a human being capable of being?

A human being can be intelligent—oh, the sweep of the mind! Selfless—oh, the breadth of the heart! Brave—he can walk forward even into death, even into the unknown. A human being can have faith. We can trust in the goodness of things even when we are being overwhelmed. A human being can be livingly alive. We can throw ourselves joyously into all there is to do and, having done this, invent yet more.

Have you ever watched animals? Let their physical appetites be slaked, and they sleep. They can sleep twenty hours a day. Not human beings! Let our physical appetites be slaked, and our mental appetites press us on. Let our mental appetites be slaked, and our spiritual appetites press us on.

To be a human being is to be alive!

How much of a human being are you?

If you are less than you may be, then be up and about the business of life.

For the business of life is just this—to be all that you may be.

To be less than this is judgment.

And if you should come up to what you think you may be, you will find you may be yet more—oh, infinitely more!

There is no limit to what you may become—because God put in you the pattern of divinity.

Anything less?

You have not yet attained.

Are you a cheat or a liar or a thief? You might be honest.

Are you a murderer? You might be a saint or even a messiah. You might be a saver of lives, a giver of life.

Are you ignorant? You might be a philosopher, a scientist, a poet. You might be a truth finder.

You hunters and trackers, do you think that your hounds pant after the hare?

If you but knew how the human mind pants after truth, once it sets upon that track! If you but knew how the human heart pants after selflessness, once it sees that it may reach even to that!

You are what you are—vicious if you are vicious, though you are swathed in the white robes of virtue! brutal if you are brute, though your friends accept you as a gentleman! false if you are false, though you sit upon the judge's bench!

It does not make any difference whether others are aware of how far you fall short of your human potential. It does not make any difference whether you are aware of how far you fall short. You still fall short!

A jackal is a jackal. I feel sure he does not know what he

is—but there he is, a jackal.

And a true man is a true man. It does not make any difference whether he knows it or not. It does not make any difference whether anyone else knows it or not. There he is—a true man!

Because we are good

Life does not have to be a scrabbling and clawing at crumbling walls—a piglike rooting and scrambling for pleasure—a clutching for handholds—a blind striking out in a black night.

Life can be what it was meant to be for us.

The person who lives like a brute, shut in by his own littleness—that person lives in a pit. This is the Pit! the bottomless pit of self.

But one day—in this lifetime or another—he looks up. There, there high above him, is a vision of another kind of life.

Then he is aware that he lives in a pit. When a person becomes aware of his shortcomings, he has taken the first step out.

You cruelest of criminals, why do you always seek to justify yourself, even your worst acts?

Not because you want people's good opinion. This you may despise.

Not because of conscience. This you may lack.

But because at heart you feel that you are good, and you must justify yourself at heart.

If human beings were truly wicked, they would feel no

need to justify themselves. No more would be expected of them, and they would expect no more of themselves. But they do!

I do not believe there is anyone, no matter how mean, who does not feel in his essential nature that he is good.

People are good, and they act only from good motives.

The Grand Inquisitor, the murderous thief, the embezzler, the tyrant slaughtering millions of innocents, the liar, the adulterer—inquire of his soul why he did it, and he will tell you, "I did it for good!"

The good may not be your notion of good; it may be a good that the whole world—except this one person—would proclaim to be evil. It may be a good that he himself—later on—will admit was evil.

But when he was acting, he was acting from good. He was trying to destroy what he considered to be hateful and bad; he was trying to improve his condition or the condition of others.

People commit crimes, get drunk, take drugs—for the same reason that they paint the Sistine Chapel, invent an electric light, or set a child's bone. They are trying to make life better. They are trying to eliminate pain, trying to increase happiness, perhaps only their own happiness, perhaps the happiness of some special group or class or nation or race. Some of the cruelest acts have been committed in the name of a people or a race or a nation, and perhaps the cruelest of all in the name of God and for His glory!

Hatred can make evil deeds look like reasonable and righteous actions.

I do not believe that we go to Hell because we commit evil deeds. We commit evil deeds because we are in Hell. We find ourselves in prison, and we think that we can break down the door that will let us out.

"I can smash my way to my good," we think. "I can make off with good by force."

Many people believe this; most of us at times; certainly many more than are in prisons.

But it does not work. For the only way out of the pit is love. The only way out of the pit is truth. The harder we beat at the walls, the more we drag them down.

Yet we have to keep on.

Why? Because we are good, and we have to keep on until we find the good.

Our spirit is like water

A Chinese philosopher once said he did not believe that human beings are naturally either good or bad. Our spirit is like water, he taught; it will run to the north or to the south, to the east or to the west.

The great teacher Mencius, upon hearing him, agreed that our spirit was like water; only, while it was true that water would run east or west, north or south, there was one direction it always ran; that was downward. Our spirit also has one direction that it always takes; that is toward the good.

Like Mencius, I believe that human beings are naturally good.

One of the reasons why I think we are good is that I have never gotten to know anyone well but that I loved him, and the better I knew him, the better I loved him.

When we see only the superficial self and surface actions of a person, we may like him or not. But when we get to know him well, get to see his secret springs of action, we always like him.

We may not condone his actions, but we do not condemn the person.

Why?

Because the deeper our knowledge of a person goes, the closer we come to his real self. The real self is good.

If I got to know you, I know that I would feel that you are good.

I do not mean that I would always find your actions good. But I do not think you always find them good either.

This is one of the reasons why I believe we are good: We know that our actions are not always good, and we have a sense of shame, a sense of falling short. If a person did not think that essentially he was good, he would have no such feeling. What would there be to fall short of?

Everyone I have ever known, no matter how much he may have accomplished, has had this feeling of falling short. This makes me think that we are not only good, we are better than anything we can even imagine ourselves to be.

In the pattern of greatness

Working always at the core of our nature is the impulse to be more than we have been.

This is why, no matter what we achieve, there is always disappointment in it. Nothing we can do, no matter how good, is ever good enough.

Did I write a song? It was not like the one I heard in my heart. Did you do a brave and generous act? It was not as heroic or selfless as you really are.

The man who designed the Taj Mahal saw flaws in its alabaster beauty that no one else could see. He had a Taj Mahal in his mind, and the one that was built out of marble, incomparable though it was, could not compare with this.

Not one of us has fulfilled our potentialities. We hardly know what they are. But we know that they are in us. There is a goodness in us we have never come close to attaining.

It may be that goodness is hardly the name for it. Certainly it has nothing to do with "goodiness."

It is a lion's goodness as much as a lamb's, a serpent's as much as a dove's. It includes destroying as well as creating, tearing down as well as building up. It is perfecting of body and all the powers of the body. It is perfecting of mind and all the gifts of the mind. It is perfecting of spirit.

In our hearts we feel that we are meant for greatness, for lofty thoughts and massive achievements, and we are. In the pattern of greatness we were shaped; the dream of greatness nurtured us through childhood and youth; if later we relinquished this dream, it was with disappointment. The American faith that every child can be President is not infantile— and America will not be better off for giving it up.

Every person is as extraordinary as the President. Every person is unique. There has never been anything else just like you and never will be. There has never been any creature more important and never will be. Everything else takes its meaning from you, in a sense. You are the center of a world—your own, it is true, but is there any more meaningful? Up and down, near and far, past and future have meaning only as they relate to you. The universe is not complete without you; without you it would not be as much. God is not complete without you. The Infinite needs you; without you it would be less than infinite. The pattern every person was formed in is of no mean size.

What have we done or been? We can surpass it. Has someone run a four-minute mile? We will run a three-minute mile. Has someone flown at a thousand miles an hour? We will fly at the speed of light—nay, at the speed of thought.

Have some been brave, so brave that you have wept at the story of their deeds? All shall be as brave.

Have some been selfless, so selfless that you have wondered if they might be gods instead of human beings? All shall be as selfless.

Have some been intelligent, so intelligent that you have marveled at their reach of mind? All shall be as intelligent.

We were born to be giants, though we may have become pygmies. We are all strivers, all going forward, and all better than we think. There is less distance between the meanest and mightiest than we may imagine. If I surpass you at this, you surpass me at that.

I have never met anyone who was not my superior at something—and I have never met anyone who could excel me at everything. None of us has a right to be proud, save as we are all proud together—proud of our humanness. For as human beings we were meant for excellence in all things.

Aim beyond your reach

We have much to overcome—in the world and in ourselves. But this does not mean we are not good.

When a sculptor carves a statue out of stone, the stone resists his chisel, but the sculptor does not call the stone evil. He knows that it is good, for through it he will bring forth something beautiful.

Each of us is a sculptor; each of us is carving a life and a soul, not out of stone but out of the living stuff of Spirit, which takes much more skill to work than stone.

Now sometimes we may seem like children struggling with a crude lump of modeling clay. But if we are children, we are children of God, of good. We are not children of darkness, but of light.

It is not expected of a child that he always hit the mark. Do not feel proud if you always hit the mark with ease. It can only mean that you are not aiming high enough.

One of the reasons why I feel that we are good is that we are forever aiming beyond our reach. We would be more than we are—yes, even a god. This is not a blasphemous wish, for it is God who planted the god-seed in our soul. The Bible says,

"Ye are gods; and all of you are children of the most High."

It is not wrong to try to build a stairway to Heaven. Though our labors lift us only a step higher, by our step all are a step higher.

How good, how gentle we can be

The wonder is not how often we fall short, but how often we measure up. It is not amazing that we do selfish acts; it is amazing how many selfless acts we do. How often we might be brutes and are not! We do all sorts of things any animal would consider foolish—and they would be foolish for an animal.

There are the Jains in India and the lengths they go to in their reverence for life; there is the eighty-year-old woman I saw planting a seedling oak in front of her house; there are the nuns who spend their lives nursing lepers; there are the soldiers who volunteer for missions from which there can be no return; there is the American doctor who gave himself a dread African disease because he knew no other way to get it into this country for the research he believed necessary for its eradication.

O the multitudes of good people!

O Jesus!

O Socrates, Gandhi, Mother Teresa!

O Galileo, Confucius, Bruno, Lincoln!

O you the unknown soldiers, not in the wars of men against men, but of man against the darkness! you who had the courage to stand and O all you silent, patient torchbearers who have carried the light forward in our long progression! you countless millions who have been decent, kind, tolerant, just, charitable!

O mothers who give yourselves for your children!

O teachers who stand back so that your students may step forward!

O you in the laboratories and hospitals who have sacrificed self for selflessness!

O you of power who have used your power in moderation, who were strong but gentle in your strength!

O all self-restrainers!

O you who refuse to do the wrong thing! you honest ones! you law-affirming ones who have made the human community possible!

O you who have refused to settle for less than the best you were capable of!

O craftsmen! you who have worked not for a price but out of pride in your product!

O you who have been true to truth!

O you who have labored to make beautiful the things you have touched!

O all strivers! you who have not shirked responsibility!

O you who have been stronger than pain, who have not let it keep you from making your contribution!

O you who have turned your defeats into triumphs of spirit!

How brave, how noble, how generous, how gentle human beings can be!

The image of the Infinite

Sometimes people speak disparagingly of human nature. "That's more than you can expect of human nature," they say, as if human nature were weak and brutish.

But what is human nature? Human nature is the most extraordinary nature we know about; there are no limits to what it can do.

What are the limits of a human being?

Human beings can outspeed an antelope, outsing a mockingbird, outclimb a squirrel, outfight a lion, outfly an eagle, outdig a mole, outswim a fish, outlift an elephant. There is no element we have not made conquests in, including the element of ourselves. More independent than a cat, we are more devoted to the welfare of our community than an ant is to its anthill. More diligent than a beaver, we can find more joy in play than an otter. More solitary than a serpent, we can delight more in company than any herd of sheep.

How then shall we limit human nature?

The body is supple, strong, complex, resilient, hard to

hurt, quick to repair itself, able to adapt to different environments. With our hands we can level mountains or dissect molecules. With our eyes we can view galaxies or probe atoms. Even as an animal, what a superb animal; no other creature can excel at so many feats.

A person's mind can soar or probe. It is imaginative, logical, sensitive. It can observe facts and arrive at principles, perceive causes and predict effects. It can detect illusion and experience truth. It can solve problems and change things. With it we are remaking the world. It is life's highest achievement; for through it life becomes conscious of itself and can determine the direction it will go. And it can go as high as God.

And oh, the spirit of Man! It contains within it abysses and peaks of joy and beauty, passion and compassion, stirrings, aspirations, powers. It can share the vicissitudes of the many, yet be one with the oneness of the One. It can reach such heights of love that it can cry from the Cross where it gives itself to all, "Father, forgive them; for they know not what they do."

How shall I define you, O Man? Where shall I place the limits upon you? Is this you? Is that you? Now do I have you? If I set these as your bounds, will you go no further?

No matter how I would define you and limit you, can I ever say else but, "Not this! Not that!" Yet if I could touch the perfect essence of being, invisible and indivisible, changeless, eternal, undetermined, indefinable, then, at last, might I not declare, "That art thou!"

O Man, you are made in the image of the Infinite!

Something better than I dream

The cells of my body perform their individual labors in order that I, a man, may exist. I doubt if any cell can comprehend what it is like to listen to a symphony or discover a law of nature or look at a star or love one's country. Yet because I am, all the cells of my body have significance, a different order of significance than they could have as cells.

So it is with me. I serve a higher order of being, a higher order of meaning. For life means more than anything anyone has imagined. Something better than I dream has made the world and made me better than I dream.

Because now I am as a child and see in "a glass, darkly," I cannot understand the whole meaning. But I know what the sea is like, though I have only stood on the shore and gazed at its expanse. I know what the sky is like, though I have never flown but only yearned upward in my heart.

Now I can only call the meaning *God.* But that is a wonderful word.

Another word for it is *Good.*

It is more than I am, as I am more than my cells. But the meaning is in Eternal Mind, and that Mind is in me. God is the infinite Fire, but I am a divine spark.

God did not make me as I might make a pot or a poem, perhaps with flaws. I am a living creature and I grow.

What have I done? It does not matter. It is nothing to what I will do. What have I been? It does not matter. It gives hardly an inkling as to what I will become. Did we not know it to be fact, which of us could believe that a caterpillar would become a butterfly?

God made me out of His will to good, out of His joy in

beauty, out of His love for living. And so I have in me a striving for perfection and a heart of love. I am good because God is good. God made me in His image.

life before this and after

NINE

The work of love and intelligence

I believe that the world is the work of a Divine Love and a Divine Intelligence, which for want of a better word I call God.

God may be more than Love—but He cannot be less. Anything less is unthinkable. If the world is not the work of Love, it is not the work of anything; it is blind chance stumbling over blind chaos.

Even I put love into my world as far as I am able to—imperfectly because I do not yet know how to love more—but God is Perfect Love.

Therefore, the world must be the perfect work of Perfect Love. It may be more—but it cannot be less.

The world must be the work of Perfect Intelligence too (for God—by the only definition worthy of the name—must be Perfect Intelligence as well as Perfect Love).

The world, then, is not put together bunglingly, but is shaped as Perfect Intelligence would shape a world it made. The Potter did not make some of his pots with flaws!

We look at the world, and at a glance we see much that does not look perfect. The world has sickness and pain in it. The world has loneliness and growing old in it. The world has loss and tears in it. The world has wounds and death in it. In this world we do not always get what we want and we do not always want what we get.

If it is a good world, then the pain must be there for a purpose—because it leads to good—a greater good than we would come to without it. The pain must be there because it is necessary—and will be there only as long as it is necessary.

To believe that the world and life and you are the good

work of a good God, you have to believe two things to be true.

One: You are immortal.

Two: Something in you—call it what you may—draws your own life to you.

A single page, a single chord

Yesterday was a cold, rainy morning. I woke sick and full of pain. I stayed in bed all day. When night fell, the rain was still coming down, and I was still full of pain. When I fell asleep, I had known only pain and misery all day long.

Today I woke restored. It was a bright, sunlit morning, and I rose rejoicing. Full of vigor, I filled my day with exciting experiences. Now in the evening I lie down, happy and content, ready for rest.

Suppose we had no memory from day to day. Suppose we only lived one day at a time.

How unjust yesterday's life was! How fortunate today's! And both meaningless happenstance.

But I know that I was sick yesterday because of things that had happened the day before, and I was well today because of what I did yesterday. Yesterday and today have meaning because I see them in sequence and in a larger frame of reference.

We never judge the events of a single day solely in the light of that day. Every day takes its meaning from its yesterdays and tomorrows, and I can live it to the full—endure it, as may be, or enjoy it, as may be—because I see it as part of my life.

Today I may have had nothing to eat, and the pangs of

hunger may seem almost unbearable as I watch my friends at their meals. But my hunger becomes very bearable when I know that it is necessary so that I may qualify for a contest tomorrow.

Today I may even be undergoing surgery. But this is bearable because I know that tomorrow I will have greater health.

A single chord—dissonant or consonant—may make no meaning, except when it is listened to from the viewpoint of a symphony.

A single page—interesting or uninteresting—may make no meaning, except when it is read from the viewpoint of a book.

So a single event may make no meaning, except when it is seen from the viewpoint of a day. A single day may make no meaning, except when it is seen from the viewpoint of a life. And a single life may make no meaning, except when it is seen from the viewpoint of a progression of lives, the viewpoint of eternity.

If we are immortal, all the events of our life are seen in a different light, in a different frame of reference.

In terms of this life, things happening to me may seem meaningless and miserable, but in terms of immortal life, they may seem very meaningful.

I woke this morning in a wood. I have toiled uphill and downhill all day. I have passed through thickets, forded streams, dallied in pleasant meadows. It has rained a little, and the sun has shone. I have seen a few wild beasts and encountered a few natural obstacles, some not easy to surmount. I have found paths I could follow, and have made paths that someone else can follow. I have met others in the wood; some of them walked with me for a way.

Now dark is coming down and the wood still stretches around me. I am weary and I ache. I cannot go much farther.

But what a difference it makes if, as I throw myself down, I feel in my heart, "This is the end. When I fall asleep, I shall not rise again"—or if I feel, "Tomorrow I shall wake refreshed and restored, eager for another day!"

Suppose I even feel, "I know that the journey I am making is long and hard, but it is a great journey—greater because it is long and hard. It is a valiant journey. It is a joyous journey. Because I make it, not only do I grow stronger, but I help others to be stronger. Not only am I better, but the world is better."

Then the journey becomes not a tragic mischance, but a divine adventure.

This is the human condition.

I have risen on innumerable mornings.

I have slept through innumerable nights.

I have journeyed on innumerable journeys.

I have lived in familiar and unfamiliar worlds.

I have had brave and beautiful companions, lovely friends.

I shall have them yet again.

I have been weak and strong, wise and unwise.

I have come on much curious knowledge, some remembered, some forgotten.

I have done many deeds, some worthy, some unworthy.

What I am undertaking I am not sure—but somehow I am sure it is an enterprise worthy of my effort.

Where I am going I am not sure—but I am sure it is a destination worthy of myself.

Here I am at this place on this day.

Tonight I shall lie down once more to sleep, and tomorrow I shall rise again and journey on.

To believe we are immortal

You may ask, Is there any reason to believe we are immortal? But I ask, Is there any reason to believe we are not?

No one has ever come up with a shred of evidence that proves we are not immortal. As to our immortality, there have been thousands—probably millions—of reports from people who have believed they have communicated with those who are dead. I am not referring to reports from spiritualists and mediums, but just ordinary people who have lost someone they loved and had an experience that convinced them their dead were there. The files of psychical research groups—most of which are run by honest, intelligent people interested in finding out what does or does not occur—bulge with such histories.

Most of the people who have such experiences never write them down. They are not writers, and they are not interested in psychical research or spiritualism. They cherish the experience themselves and perhaps on occasion relate it to a friend.

Such reports are of necessity unverified, for who is there to verify them? And who is there to deny them? If I tell you I have had a message from another world, will you travel there to find out if I have? or will I?

There are many experiences in life that are not effectively communicated; they are too subjective. If I try to tell you about such a simple thing as a cup of coffee on a cold morning, it is easy to get you to share my experience if you have ever had it; almost impossible if you have not. My words leave out the flavor—and the essence is in the flavor.

So it is with experiences like this. When it happens to you, the event produces so vivid an impression that it leaves you shaking, your very bones quivering with the intense reality; yet when you go to recount it to me, what you communicate is flat and dull and may leave me wondering what really happened.

No one can make another believe that he has spoken with his dead. But if you ever have, no one—not all the theologians, philosophers, and scientists in this world—can make you believe that you have not.

And all you scientists who tell me it only happened to me in my mind, can you tell me one thing that did not?

Every person feels he or she is immortal

Another reason for believing you are immortal is also a subjective one. It is simply that every person feels he or she is immortal.

I do not believe—and I think that psychologists bear this out—that we ever truly feel that we will come to an end.

You are an immortal self. Each person knows this. Each person feels this. Even suicides know it; perhaps this is why they can commit suicide; they know they cannot destroy their self.

In our hearts we do not feel we can be destroyed. Our body can be destroyed; our mind can be taken from us; but our self—we cannot conceive of this coming to an end.

My own experience with the dying has made me feel that

body and mind are a kind of bridge by which we cross over into the world and out of it again. By it we communicate with others on this mind-body plane we call our world.

Beyond body, beyond mind, beyond thinking, beyond living and dying, there is the self.

My self uses mind and uses body; it lives in and through them; it can withdraw from them. This, too, I know—when it withdraws from them, it goes back through a door you cannot find, search as you may. Death is a wall that has no opening from this side. My self knows where the door is, but mind and body cannot find it.

It is a door in a looking-glass kind of world. Clear enough, I believe, from one side; but from the other, not there at all.

You do not believe such a thing can be! Of course not—how can you? But there it is.

Logic is a way of looking at things—and a good way; it works beautifully in a mind-body world. I think it is the slide rule God used in laying this world out. But do not expect it to work in other worlds; it does not even work here for lovers or believers. And I have a feeling—not a particularly logical feeling, but not illogical either—that in infinity there is every conceivable kind of world and every inconceivable kind too.

The world is not what we think it is at all; it is infinitely more. If we get to thinking we know all the answers, it only means we have not asked many questions. The world is stranger and more lovely and more meaningful than any meaning or loveliness we may attach to it.

And so are we.

More than he values life

I believe Man is immortal because he has to live as if he were.

The life that values only this life is not the best of all possible lives, but the poorest.

If this life were the only life we had, surely its preservation would be the highest conceivable good. We would put this above everything else—far, far above everything else.

And we would put the pleasures of this life above everything else. We would want to hold on to every moment of this life and to stuff every moment of it with pleasure. What else could be considered so good? What else could be worth half as much?

And life is good—we should hold on to it. Pleasure is good—we should value it.

But merely holding on to this life has never been the highest good.

And the life devoted to pleasure turns out to be a life in which there is at last no pleasure at all.

Is this not strange, if this life is all we have?

Even by the most materialistic of standards—by the law of the survival of the fittest—we should be able to tell which attitudes and values are true by seeing which ones best fit a person to live. True attitudes are life-supporting; false attitudes, life-destroying. Survival depends on the ability to tell truth from falsehood.

But which attitudes and values are necessary if we are to survive and reach our fullest development?

They are exactly the ones we would expect to need most if this life were not the only one we had.

To survive and reach our fullest development, we have to live as if we were immortal; we have to value many things more than we value life.

And it is not the worst of us who have held life lightly when we have had to weigh it against what we thought to be of higher value. It has been the strongest, the bravest, the wisest, the best.

It was Socrates who said to his judges: "The difficulty, my friends, is not in avoiding death, but in avoiding unrighteousness; for that runs faster than death."

And the greatest Man of all said: "Father, remove this cup from me: nevertheless not my will, but thine, be done."

Is there any sight in life more moving than to see an old man planting young trees!

If the slayer thinks he slays

How often human beings hold life cheap—their own as well as that of others. This is a terror-filled as well as a wonder-filled fact.

Many have observed that it is much harder to live than to die. We die easily—and kill easily—sometimes much too easily—almost as if to say, "See how easy it is. There is nothing to fear."

We die for love of country, and from pride, and from disappointment, and for love. We give up our lives before we give up our self-respect, and we give them up to win the respect of others. We give up our lives rather than be false to what we believe to be true.

There is some part of us that knows with Krishna: "If the slayer thinks he slays, or if the slain thinks he is slain, neither of these knows the truth about himself. For the Self is never born and never dies."

Some day we shall know why we die, and when we know all the reasons, we shall see that death is a natural part of life, an incident as birth is an incident. And not a cruel and needless anguish—not anguish at all to the dying, only to the living—but a necessary kindness, man having come no further than he has now come—as kind as sleep, as darkness, as winter, as stillness.

Out of His infinite mercy, God has made the day and the night and divided them with sleep. Eternity might overwhelm us if we had to face or comprehend it all at once, but we can face it and comprehend it one day at a time, one life at a time. When we have no need of dying, we shall no longer die.

To justify the injustices

Some people are born into rich and happy families. They are brought up in a fairly secure world. They are well-educated. They have happy families of their own and rear happy children. They survive in good health for sixty, seventy, eighty years, and at last die peacefully in bed surrounded by sorrowing and admiring survivors.

Others are born starving and ill. They are brought up maimed in mind and body in a world of war and suffering. They are abandoned in their infancy. They are taught to cringe or bully. They are murdered in their youth.

How can we justify such injustices of birth?

Most of the time most of us accept our life as if it were just an accident.

We find ourselves healthy, unhealthy, poor, affluent, threatened, or secure; and we say, "It's God's will," or "It's luck," or "It's fate."

That God could will me good health and you ill health, me wealth and you poverty, me a long life and you an early death, I cannot believe. If God is, He is justice, and He treats us with equal love and equal wisdom. God is law—or God is not.

The question has to be: Is the world run by law or chance?

Is there a reason why I find myself where I am and what I am—or is this just the working out of blind chance?

To believe that this world is the good work of a good God, we have to believe there is a reason why.

If Love made the world, there has to be a reason why there is an idiot child.

There has to be a reason why there is a race of people so insanely cruel that they torture and destroy whole races of their fellow human beings.

There has to be a reason why there is a natural catastrophe that wipes out a town—small children, young men and women, old and helpless invalids, all!

To believe that this world is the good work of a good God requires us, as I have said, to believe first that we are immortal. Then we do not judge life by its momentary appearance; we know that one rainy, windy day is not all there is to spring.

Second, we have to believe that each person draws his own life to himself.

If this is a world where it is just good or ill luck that drew my life to me, then it is a meaningless world.

But if somehow I am responsible—if somehow my lot is a just one and law is at work in what my life turns out to be—if

203

I am I because this is what I have come up to, or down to!—
then it is a meaningful world.

Such a world as Love might make, such a world as Intelligence might make.

Is there reason to believe this might be such a world?

We cannot prove that it is such a world—but we can believe that it is.

We cannot prove the world is anything. Is it physical, mental, or spiritual in nature? Is it the product of chance force or of Love and Intelligence?

There is no way to prove that we are immortal.

There is no way to prove that we are not.

There is no way to prove that we draw the circumstances of our life to us; there is no way to prove that we do not.

But to me, the only kind of world I can see any meaning in is a world where we are immortal and draw to ourselves the circumstances we find ourselves in.

And I find it impossible to believe that the world does not have meaning—even though the meaning may be beyond my power to comprehend.

We have to believe that this present life is just one episode in a life that began long, long before we were born and will end only long, long after we die—when, we cannot say, but not before we have completed ourselves—or there is not a shred of justice in the whole sorry business.

You may believe that it is not necessary for there to be justice—or what we would consider justice—in a world as vast and nonhuman as this appears to be.

Certainly God does not have to account to me for His actions. I cannot bring Him to the question—not because it is blasphemy to try, as some think—but because I do not know how.

God gave me this mind to ask questions with—of Him and everything else—but my mind has only progressed to simple fractions, and to understand God's answers I need the calculus, differential and integral—and infinite.

Now I can only guess at what God is like and what He is about.

But I believe that God gave me a mind capable of telling right from wrong and justice from injustice.

When I see people born with little chance to have any but a maimed and miserable life—spiritually, mentally, and physically—and others born into a world where they will have little chance to have any but a full and happy life— spiritually, mentally, and physically—it is going to take a lot of talking by God or anyone else to convince me that this is just.

A world where this little life we see is all the life we have, a world into which people are born into such unequal conditions—such a world is too unjust for me to believe God would have made it.

Therefore, I have to believe that this little life I now have is but an episode in my total life, which began before I got here and will go on when I have left here. And I have to believe also that the conditions I find myself in are conditions I somehow drew to myself.

We have lived before

If I accept the fact that we have lived before, then the injustices of birth, the seemingly inexplicable differences that exist between people and their conditions in life, can be accepted and, if not explained, at least understood.

How else can you account for such differences?

One morning we wake to see a man dragged out into the town square and shot. We see another called out and awarded a medal.

Suppose each day was a complete life and we had no memory of anything before or after. To us, the first man would have been just born—and immediately killed. The second man would have been just born—and immediately honored. What an unjust procedure we would feel we had witnessed!

But we happen to know that the first man murdered his neighbor last week, and yesterday the second man won a contest. So these events, instead of being the inexplicable caprice of fortune, become understandable to us.

We look at a child of nine months and think of him as different from a man of ninety.

We see things happen to him that perplex and horrify us—or fill us with delight at his good fortune.

If we saw them happen to a man of ninety, we would understand and accept them as reasonable.

But perhaps the child of nine months is reaping what he sowed for ninety years—or even nine hundred years.

By sowing and reaping I do not mean that we are rewarded and punished for what we have done. I do not believe that God or the world punishes and rewards. The world is an orderly world, that is all—a world where all things come to fruition, each thing after its kind. If we plant an apple, our tree bears apples; if we plant a thorn, our tree bears thorns.

But to be born in a thorn thicket out of the whim of the world, while others are born in an apple orchard! I do not believe it.

I drew the conditions of my life.

I cannot find the right word to say how I drew them.

I hardly like to say *desire,* because sometimes they are anything but what I think I desire.

I hardly like to say *choice,* because they are certainly not the work of my will.

I hardly like to say *thought,* because what I think is not enough to explain the world I find myself in—and it is not a very satisfactory word for explaining an idiot child or the extinction of a community by a tidal wave; it is difficult to believe everyone in the city was thinking the same thought.

A better word is *consciousness,* but it is such a big word.

Jesus used the word *faith*—and elsewhere in this book I have said what I thought this word means.

The East says *karma,* and it is as good a word as any. It simply means that our every thought, word, and deed from the beginning of time has left a trace on the stuff of being, shaping and limiting it into the form and mind and heart that we call ourselves.

Perhaps all these words are needed because it is not any part of us but all of us that shapes our world.

There is a kind of pattern in the soul; there is a sum of thought, a composite of tendencies.

You are a pattern in a pattern. You are a totality of thoughts, feelings, impulses, needs; and it is this sum total of you, the whole person, the underlying essential nature, that becomes the magnet that shapes the field of your world and draws the things in it around you.

What makes a magnet a magnet?

When you were a child in school, did you ever set up a

magnet, sprinkle iron filings around it on a sheet of paper, and then tap the paper? The filings are drawn to the magnet and arrange themselves in definite patterns around it.

Obviously the magnet is influencing the shape of the world around it; it is setting up lines of force that determine how the things that make up the world of the magnet are going to react.

It is the same with the magnet in your soul. It sets up the field of force that is you, and it draws to you the events of your life as if they were iron filings, shaping them into the shape they assume.

A world governed by law

It is interesting that all people in a state of nature assume they have lived before; they accept reincarnation as a fact. I am not certain, but I believe that anthropologists have never found any primitive people who did not believe this.

And almost all civilized people believe in reincarnation. For ages on ages, by far the greater part of the human race has accepted this belief as the most reasonable of all explanations as to what occurs after death. It accounts for the conditions of this life on earth and provides a means by which living creatures can grow and unfold into perfection.

Almost all the people who have lived in Asia have believed in reincarnation, and countless Europeans and Americans, from Pythagoras and Socrates and Plato to Goethe and Edison and Jung.

I do not myself say: reincarnation. I just say: continuing life. Life before this one and after it. And by life, I mean a process not too unlike this one, a way of existence where we change and grow.

Exactly where, exactly how, here on this earth, or elsewhere in the unfolding universe—does it matter?

Are we reborn at once? How long an interval passes between death and birth? Where does the soul wander during all this time?

I do not pretend to know. But what is time except in a world of time?

How long a time passes between falling asleep and waking again? If it were not for sunset and sunrise, for clocks and friends to tell the passing hours, would sleep take any time at all?

How long is a dream that lasts for half a second but embraces half a lifetime?

You have come up to here. And what are you encountering now—is it not such that you can trust what brought you this far to see you further on your way?

I am responsible for my lot in life. If fortunate, somehow I drew it. If unfortunate, somehow I drew that.

If I am responsible, then let me be about changing it.

And though it may not be enough to say that our thinking is responsible for the conditions of our life, it is clear that it is in our thinking we have to begin to change. There is no other starting place.

When we do change our thinking—this I know—the conditions in our life change.

If you find your condition in life an unhappy one, you may wonder how and why.

No one knows this now. Psychologists are beginning to examine the mechanisms by which thought processes become body processes—become a disease, for instance, or a cure for one—but they are only beginning.

Some day we will know the laws involved and be better able to control the processes.

For what happens to you is the result of the working of laws. Believe nothing less.

The more we learn about our world, the more we see that law rather than chance governs it.

Our fathers thought that almost everything was the result of blind force or the whim of the gods.

But our age has been the age of the discovery of laws. Whatever field our scientists have investigated, they have discovered that it is governed, not as men previously had believed, by chance, but by law.

Everywhere we see an orderly process; smaller and smaller grow the areas that we still believe are governed by chance.

This is a world governed by law—and in a world governed by law, we and our life come under law too.

What the laws will be we may not yet know, but we will know. For now, it is enough to call them the law of mind action, which is to say that what you think and desire and speak and believe in your heart, that you become!

it all makes sense

TEN

Why we have the life we have

As to why we have the life we now have, we are complex beings; many and complex would be the forces at work through who knows how many lives to push us in this direction and that to where we now are.

But there are a number of possible explanations that reason might advance as to why some people have handicaps and hard conditions in their lives.

I have known many people who were able to adjust to life if they only had to meet it partway. They foundered when they tried to put out into the deep, but could live happily on the shore—though they always looked with longing at the sea.

I think that sometimes souls are not ready for this life— they resist coming into it—they refuse, as it were, to be born. In a sense, they say, "I may have to live, but I shall live as little as possible."

We all do this at times during life—we have to hide from it occasionally or can meet it only partway. Why is it not reasonable to think we do so at its inception?

We are born with the hunger for living, but we hunger, too, for dying. We have the urge to keep going, but also we want to lie down. If we stay awake long enough, there is nothing we long for like sleep.

In a sense, I suppose, we all commit suicide, even those who love life most.

Some do it slowly, little by little, and some all at once.

Primitive people believe it is natural to live forever. We were made to be immortal. There is no natural death—only witchcraft or violence can bring us to an end.

I think they are right—only the witchcraft is one we work against ourselves.

We die from an inward necessity that draws us to our end. We do not enlist, we are drafted. But the conscripting officers are not those of chance; they are impulses, drives, motivations in our own soul.

This life is a sea journey.

But it is not a journey we all want to make.

Some of us feel in our souls like shanghaied sailors.

Some of us make the journey, but we do it in the sick bay or the brig.

Some of us jump ship at the first port of call.

Some of us even leap overboard.

On the other hand, perhaps we have come to the place in our unfoldment where we need to develop a quality that only an extraordinary challenge will give us the opportunity to develop.

I know no way to be brave except to face fear. If I must walk forward even into death or stand firm against the taunts of the whole human society, then I must walk forward or stand firm.

If, in order to learn to love, I must sell all that I have and give it to the poor, then sell I must.

This I know: Something in me delights in difficulties. I am most alive, not when everything is easiest, but when everything is hardest.

Man lives at the cutting edge of life.

Resilient, bold, vigorous, he grows at the timberline of the world.

And he was meant to grow.

Life is effort. To be human takes the hardest kind of effort.

But it is worth the effort.

Life is effort

Life is effort—but life is worth the effort.

Life makes sense, and everything in it makes sense.

What comes to us comes because we draw it to us; somehow it is ours to face and wrestle with. We have made an appointment with it, and there it is.

The salmon are drawn from the deep to the stream where they were born; and we are drawn to the life we find ourselves in—not by chance—but because here is our place to grow and fulfill ourselves, to reach the ends for which we were born.

Some have many hard things to bear in life and go down under them. But some go down—and spring back.

When I first moved into the place where I now live, growing outside my window was a cherry tree, aged, stunted, twisted, black.

One stormy night this miserable little tree broke off at the ground. When I examined the stump, I found it crawling with termites.

So I hacked the stump back into the ground and poured creosote over and through and around the remains.

I then forgot the tree. But when spring came, up from that mutilated, tortured stump a twig appeared, and the twig grew into a stem, and the stem put forth branches and leaves.

I asked a nurseryman if he thought there was any chance that the thing would live and bear fruit.

"None at all," he said. "It is valueless. Chop it down."

But I did not chop it down.

That has now been many years. The little tree did not die. It grew.

All the years I have lived here, I have picked cherries from it—red, delicious, perfect cherries, at least enough for a pie or two.

If it were an orchard of cherry trees, it could not give so much to me; for the little tree glows life-colored in my heart, and even more than cherries, I have gathered courage from it.

"Life is stronger than death," says the tree. "Whatever appearances may be, never accept them."

You must only keep on!

You must always keep on.

This is life's message to all living things.

Keep on. Keep on. Keep on.

You must never give up.

Pray on. Struggle on. Fight on. Work on. Walk on. Dream on.

Keep on.

A thousand difficulties, a thousand prophets will arise to dissuade you from your purpose and to thwart your enterprise.

Only keep on.

You may fall. You may fail.

You may fall a thousand times.

It shall not matter if you get up and go on toward the goal.

Life does not measure you by what you did not do; it only measures you by what you do.

You there, the runner in the race, have you fallen a thousand times and still you hold the record? It is you who wears the crown; it is you they carry home upon their shoulders.

It is not entered in the books how many times you fell; it is only entered that you won the race.

It is easy never to fail. Never try to be more.

Be content with your powers and achievements; be content with what you have become.

No, you still will fail. For you start to fail whenever you stop trying to succeed.

You cannot stand still. You are alive. And life cannot stand still; to stay alive, life has to grow. If you are not pressing forward, you are slipping back.

You cannot rest content for long.

You can loaf for an hour or two. Perhaps even a day or two. You can sleep for a night. But lie abed for a week, and your muscles begin to wither away. Lie still long enough and you lose the power to move.

You do not gain energy by conserving it.

The way to have more energy is to use the energy you have. The way to have more strength is to use the strength you have.

There is nothing wrong with failing.

I have failed hundreds of times. I wonder if there is anyone alive who has not failed hundreds of times, in private and in public endeavors.

How many things I have wanted to do but could not do!

How many things I have wanted not to do yet have done!
How many things I have had to try to do over and over again
before I could do them!

Every person falls short every day of his or her life. What a
pitiful life it would be if one did not!

A person's failures may be a better measure of his stature
than his successes.

One can succeed if one does not aim very high.

Which one failed—he who climbed to the top of the
green knoll of summer or he who fell not halfway to the
crest of the ice-encrusted peak beyond the clouds?

This is the reason for life—to aim and to stretch and to
reach.

To grow.

What have you thought and done?

What have you thought and not done?

Even more than this you will do.

There have always been many to say, "It is hopeless." Yet
after a million years or more of chance and change, of
fortune and misfortune, we human beings still pursue our
great and perilous adventure.

If in the end the world comes tumbling down, I hope I
shall hear, across the tumult of the falling stars, some Roland
of that unimagined age blowing his deathless horn at
Roncesvalles, blowing his defiance of all that is less than
might have been, blowing his faith that the good will triumph yet.

A fish not even gold

Do not give up. Keep on.

I may not know who will win the race, but I know who will lose it—it will be those who did not keep on till the end.

There is such a thing as second wind—and there is such a thing as divine help—and it comes to those who keep on.

A few years ago in my garden I built two shallow lily ponds and put goldfish into them. They multiplied. But dogs tore the liner and ruined the ponds, so in the fall I drained them and gave away the fish.

Later that fall much rain fell and in the winter, much snow. Two or three inches of water formed in the bottom of the pools. It must have been frozen solid for at least a month and must have frozen solid and thawed a number of times. There may have been times when the pools were dry.

When spring came I went out one Sunday afternoon to measure the pools, as I intended to rebuild them. I measured the larger pool, then went to the smaller one. It had no water in it. It had rained a week before, so how long it had been dry I do not know. There were a few spots of half-dry, oozy muck in the bottom.

On top of this muck, in the sun, on its side and not breathing, lay a goldfish about three inches long.

I still remember my surprise at seeing it, there in the middle of that empty pond, shining in the sun, a little red-gold fish. "It has to be dead," I thought. But almost as I thought it, something in that fish said, "No, no, I am alive. Pick me up."

I ran to the house and got a glass of water.

I picked up the fish—and it gasped!

I put it in the glass and for a long time it did not move again. I could see that one fin was gone and part of its side was damaged.

I moved the fish from the glass into a larger bowl. For several days it showed almost no sign of life, but little by little its vitality came back, and in a week that little fish was lashing with life. That fish was the most alive creature I ever saw. He spent every waking moment flashing, darting, hurtling around that bowl and trying to push through the glass.

When I put him back in the lily pond, he lived in it as if he knew how dear life is and he was not going to waste a moment of it.

How had he survived that winter of freezing and thawing and drying out? It is hard to surmise.

And what if I had not gone out to the pond on that March day? A few more minutes at most and he must have died.

But he lived—lived to live furiously again!

You may not think so, but I will always believe I had to go out to that pond because he had to live.

I suppose you had to see my fish to understand. You had to pick him up. You had to see him lashing about that bowl. You had to see him whirling through that pond.

Somehow that fish had the livingness of life in him.

What a fuss to make about a fish, you may be saying, and a ridiculous coincidence!

Perhaps, but O God and all of you dear friends who have read my book, I am only such a fish, not even gold. And my pond is also a perilous, precarious place; it, too, has had many times of freezing, of thawing, and of drying out.

And like my fish, I, too, am here; I feel, because I have called, and the feet of the world have been no less swift when they ran to succor me.

We are all linked, one to another. We answer, though we have heard no voice. We respond, though we do not know we have been summoned.

And the universe responds to us—with powers you could not think were there, by ways you had no forethought of, bringing help you could not know would come.

The water comes down at Niagara Falls

The water comes down at Niagara Falls like nothing else I know of on this earth.

This is no spidery tissue of a cataract; you cannot even call it a torrent. A massive river—the entire Great Lakes—disgorges over high, wide cliffs and plunges almost two hundred feet!

Niagara Falls is power.

Sheer, raw power.

However you experience it—whether you stand where the wide, smooth expanse of placid river suddenly convulses into a churning rapids; whether you go down into the Cave of the Winds underneath the foaming precarious wall of water and rock or ride the *Maid of the Mist* out into the slavering, pounding gorge; or whether you stand at Prospect Point and watch the raging, howling flood hurl itself over the brink—thunder, thunder, thunder!—shaking the earth you stand on—Niagara Falls is power.

It has been many years since I was there. I remember the power. I do not believe anyone could ever forget it.

But along with the power, I remember something else.

221

Almost at the very brink of the falls, up out of that roaring, angry chaos of water, a tree was growing.

Not a large tree, but a tree.

Somehow a seed had gotten lodged in the rocks there at the edge of doom. The seed had sprouted, put down its thin, weak tendril of root through the bitter granite, sent up its thin, weak tendril of stem through the pounding torrent, shot forth its leaves to flutter in the air like gay green sails, and there it was—a tree!

That single, silent, battered little tree had more to say to me than all that noisy, mighty, overwhelming force that is the falls.

That tree was life.

And seeing it, somehow I had a sense of what life is about.

I do not mean that I understood the reason for life. If there was anything that had no reason for being, it was that tree growing out of that maelstrom. This was the last place for a tree—if trees were reasonable and had to have a reason for being.

But the tree did not have to have a reason for being there.

The tree was its own reason for being.

The tree was a green life putting out leaves to flutter in the breezes and soak up the sun—flowering, forming seeds to shower upon the air and river, growing taller and sturdier from season to season, resting and waiting too, occasionally a haven for flying insects and birds, if any were brave enough to fly above that wild uproar—in short, a living tree!

If all the philosophers who have ever philosophized and all the poets who have ever poetized could have uttered with one voice the greatest truths they have ever uttered, they would not have said as much to me about life as that silent tree.

For the tree was life.

Life, going about doing what it is always going about doing—living, growing, becoming, being!

For a moment I looked down into the black, howling maw of the world, and there I saw the green tree of life growing right out of the midst of it—and I was not afraid.

For suddenly I knew that that green tree of life is always going to be growing there. And suddenly I knew that that green tree of life is always going to be growing in me.

I do not mean that storms may not batter it down—but if they do, it will sprout again and again.

For I sensed that this life that sends out its tender roots and stems in me, this life so frail, vulnerable, easily swept away, is the mightiest force in the world.

It spreads across the earth, across the solar system, across the Milky Way, across the nebulae scattered through the universe, across all the universes, across unimagined gulfs and immeasurable aeons, across eternities, across infinities, a Niagara of Niagaras, a force of forces, gentle, making no noise, imperceptible, patient, growing so slowly that you cannot see it growing, you can only see that it has grown, growing one cell at a time—yet filling everywhere.

Then I prayed, O green tree of life, help me understand what you mean—not in terms of meaning, but in terms of living.

For you are also a redbird singing in the winter snow, not singing for a reason, just singing to sing.

You are a caterpillar sleeping dreamlessly in your cocoon, and you will mean no more when you are a butterfly than when you were a caterpillar.

You are my cat napping under the lilac bush, and you are the lilac bush, and you are the worm gnawing at the bush.

And you are yourself.

Life does not live to prove something. Life does not have to be this or that; nothing has to be anything but what it is.

Life grows, and each thing grows after its kind.

You may be brave and wise and beautiful—and I may be none of these. But the only beauty and wisdom and courage I can have is to be true to what I have in me to be.

The tree growing in the falls does not have to be the tree growing in a forest, nor does the tree growing in the forest have to be the tree in the waterfall.

And I do not have to be you.

A tree is a tree is a tree.

A bird is a bird is a bird.

And I am I am I.

I would be your green tree, O God.

I would put forth not roots but reasonableness, not leaves but love, not a trunk but a hunger for truth, not branches but a brave seeking after God and the good. Let my flowers be friendship and a joyous spirit, and my fruit high thinking and bold action.

For we human beings are the feet of God and the hands of God and—I pray—the love of God.

It is our gift to change the world for the better, to grasp it rough and hew it beautiful.

We are shapers and doers.

We must try to grasp the thought of the world and shape it more clearly if we can. We must try to lay hold of the heart of things and shape them lovelier. And also we must lay hold of the world and things themselves, with our hands as well as with our heart and mind—seize them as a sculptor with his chisel seizes stone or a potter with his wheel turns clay or a mechanic with his tools works obdurate metals, forging, hammering, drawing forth, fastening together, trimming, adjusting until they have been formed into mighty but docile machines.

And God, I would give the gifts that are mine as naturally as a tree gives shade or a bird song.

For I am more than a tree or a bird.

This is my gift—to find the world a wilderness and leave it a garden; to come into a wasteland and build in it a city full of towers and conversation and music and visions and shining deeds; to come upon the earth and lift it up to be a star in a world of stars.

How hard it is to be human

How hard it is to be human! I know nothing harder than this—unless it is to be God! Oh, that must be a task—to have to love everyone—people and suns and stars—yes, everyone! to have to understand them and shrug off their abuse and forgive their shortcomings and listen to their cries and sense their sufferings—even a sparrow's—and help them do better and be patient when they don't even try—thank God it's God's task, that's all I can say.

To be human is hard enough—so much is asked of a human being!

We have to grow up—that means freeing others and accepting responsibility for them, all at the same time.

We have to be strong—when being strong means going without things we want and accepting things we don't want. And we have to keep on doing this—sometimes all our life.

We have to stand and do battle when we would rather run

away—and sometimes we have to run away when we would prefer to do battle.

We have to learn how to live as human beings—and there is no one to tell us what the rules of life are. We have to find them out for ourselves—and this may take most of a lifetime.

After we have found them, we have to try to live by them—and for this a lifetime is not enough for most of us.

The human task is to be the very best human being we are capable of being; to live the most alive life we can live.

To me this means:

I have to be as honest as I can.

I have to be as brave as I can.

I have to be as selfless as I can.

I have to be as cheerful as I can.

I have to work as hard as I can.

I have to think as straight as I can.

I have to use my mind and all my powers to increase on every hand life, love, beauty, power, intelligence, joy.

I have to grow!

All this is very, very hard. At least it has been for me—and I can't believe it is much easier for you.

Much of the time we do not want to be any better than we are, and even when we do, we do not know how.

We keep repeating the old errors even when we see the truth.

We are weak when we should be strong.

We are stubborn when we should be nonresistant.

Too often we find ourselves acting in no one's interest but our own; too often not even in our own!

226

But oh, the end that lies before us if we just keep at the task—the human world divine that this man-god, god-man in us can grasp and shape if he but will!

A world where the battle is not of men against men, but of man against the darkness.

A world where brutality becomes brotherhood.

A living world, a happy world, a world of works undreamed of, a world that is a fitting habitation for the human heart and mind.

A world where nations cooperate with one another—and compete with one another, not out of the craving for conquest, but like runners in a race who compete out of the desire to excel.

A world where all people have a chance to develop the potential they were born with.

A world where you and I are free to live as we will, but where we will to live for one another.

The world of which the Master dreamed when He said, "Ye are gods . . . children of the most High."

How hard it is to be human, but how thankful to be human am I!

The end of the book

You have opened my book and read.

I do not know what notions you sat down to read with, but I pray I may have made you think. For thinking is, I suppose, the mark of a human being. I pray, too, that I may have stirred and bothered you, that I may have made you feel as well as think.

For thinking of itself has never gotten anyone into the temple.

You will not get in by virtue of books—mine or anyone else's—or quotations or authorities or facts or statistics or graphs or technicalities of the law; none of these nor all of these will get you through the door.

Come from the libraries. Come from the computers. Come from the lecture halls. You must leave your cap and gown outside along with your shoes.

For in the end, you must come naked and present yourself before the doorkeeper; and he shall look into your heart and weigh it against a feather—as the Egyptian god Osiris once weighed the hearts of the dead.

But this is the temple of life, and its keeper is the living God.

Only he whose heart is very very light shall be able to get through the door this god keeps.

You will need winged thoughts.

So I have tried to turn your head and coax you into trying to fly with your wings of wax.

Do not be afraid lest you rise too near the truth.

Chapter II

Chapter VII

Chapter VIII

Chapter X